LANARKSHIRE BUSES

LANARKSHIRE BUSES

DOUGLAS G. MACDONALD

Frontispiece: An evocative shot of Baxter's Bus Services No.60 (FVD225) in Coatbridge in the early 1960s. The Leyland PD2 had been bought second-hand from neighbouring independent Irvine of Salsburgh, although new to Hutchison, Overtown along with 'sister' FVD 224.

The bus is passing the Whitelaw Fountain, a famous landmark in the Lanarkshire town. The 'Cinema' is long-gone, but the 'Odeon' building still stands, a few yards to the left of the location, albeit as a Snooker club. Under the bridge, the Shark's Mouth pub is still pulling pints for its regulars. (A.J. Douglas)

First published 2003

Tempus Publishing Limited
The Mill, Brimscombe Port,
Stroud, Gloucestershire, GL5 2QG

© Douglas G. MacDonald, 2003

The right of Douglas G. MacDonald to be identified as the Author of this work has been asserted in accordance with the Copyrights, Designs and Patents Act 1988.

All rights reserved. No part of this book may be reprinted or reproduced or utilised in any form or by any electronic, mechanical or other means, now known or hereafter invented, including photocopying and recording, or in any information storage or retrieval system, without the permission in writing from the Publishers.

British Library Cataloguing in Publication Data.
A catalogue record for this book is available from the British Library.

ISBN 0 7524 2805 5

Typesetting and origination by Tempus Publishing Limited
Printed in Great Britain by Midway Colour Print, Wiltshire

Contents

	Acknowledgements	6
	Introduction	7
one	Central Control	9
two	Baxter's – A Broth of a Bus Company!	29
three	Hutchie's Hold Over Towns	47
four	Carmichael's 'Highland' Fling	61
five	Great 'Chieftain' o' the Omnibus Race	69
six	Wilson's – 'The Wonder Years'	77
seven	'Eastern' Impact on the West	85
eight	Stokes – Smooth Operators!	93
nine	The Irvine Influence	101
ten	Clyde Valley Variety	115
eleven	Bingo Buses!	125

Acknowledgements

This work reflects a life-long interest in both public transport and local history. It realises an ambition to produce and publish photographic memories of a bygone era, and hopefully they may rekindle nostalgic thoughts in many folk, in both Lanarkshire and beyond.

The book could not have been compiled without the assistance of numerous people, acknowledged below, and to whom I extend my grateful thanks for the generosity of their time, knowledge and resources. Special credit must be registered to Alistair Douglas, for the use of many of his images, supplemented by invaluable information, and occasional correction of my errors! The photographs have come from a variety of sources, with contributors identified alongside the views they have made available for use in this volume. Many have come from my own collection, built up over three decades, and whose originators I have failed to trace, despite my best efforts. I duly apologise for the lack of proper acknowledgement in these cases.

Stewart Anderson/Donnie Ferris (Hutchison's of Overtown); Peter Irvine (Irvine of Law); Gordon Wilson; The Stokes family; Ian & John Tennant; Andrew Lindsay; James Baxter; Gerry Cushley; John Whittle; Roy Marshall; George McIntosh; Robert Williams; Arnold Richardson; Ted Jones; John Nye; Steve Kelly; Gordon Stirling; Peter Yeomans; Ray Simpson; Ken Langhorn; the Irvine family, Salsburgh; David Thomson (Golden Eagle); Robert Whiteford.

Introduction

The County of Lanarkshire's geographical location sees it at the heart of Scotland's Central Belt. Its close proximity to Glasgow and its own natural resources have given Lanarkshire an important part in the country's social and cultural history.

The Industrial Revolution impacted heavily on the area, and until their demise, Lanarkshire was renowned primarily for steel-making, engineering, and coal-mining. In sharp contrast to the grime and dust of towns like Motherwell, Wishaw and Coatbridge, the region always had its green oases and rural villages. Lanark, the county town at the head of the Clyde Valley was, and still is, an important agricultural centre.

Nowadays, local government divides Lanarkshire into 'North' and 'South', with administrative centres in Motherwell and Hamilton respectively. New technology, both manufacturing, and services, has replaced the traditional industries and on-going regeneration should help Lanarkshire cope with the twenty-first century. This book, however, deals not with the present or future, but with the past, albeit for many readers a not-so-distant past.

The era covered is from the mid-1950s to the end of the 1970s. This span captures what many consider to be the 'halcyon days' of bus operations in the county. This was a time when people were more reliant on public transport for work and play, and in the days before car ownership was almost taken as read. Links between the towns and villages of Lanarkshire and with Glasgow's metropolis as well as other parts of the country necessitated decent bus services, even more so when Dr Beeching dished out his lethal medicine to the urban and rural rail networks.

Provision during these years was principally by two companies of the nationalised Scottish Bus Group, and a whole variety of independents, many of whom no longer exist.

This volume is not an in-depth history of any or all of those operators, large or small, but is designed to be a fair, retrospective overview. The parameters have been deliberately set wide, to include companies who provided stage-carriage services, and those who served communities with workers', miners' or school buses.

It is genuinely hoped that the content, especially the photographs, will be of interest not only to bus or transport enthusiasts, but also to those who enjoy looking at nostalgic images, and, of course, to anyone with a Lanarkshire connection! The types of vehicles shown in the pictures have their own particular relevance, but the locations may also evoke memories.

Douglas G. MacDonald,
September 2003.

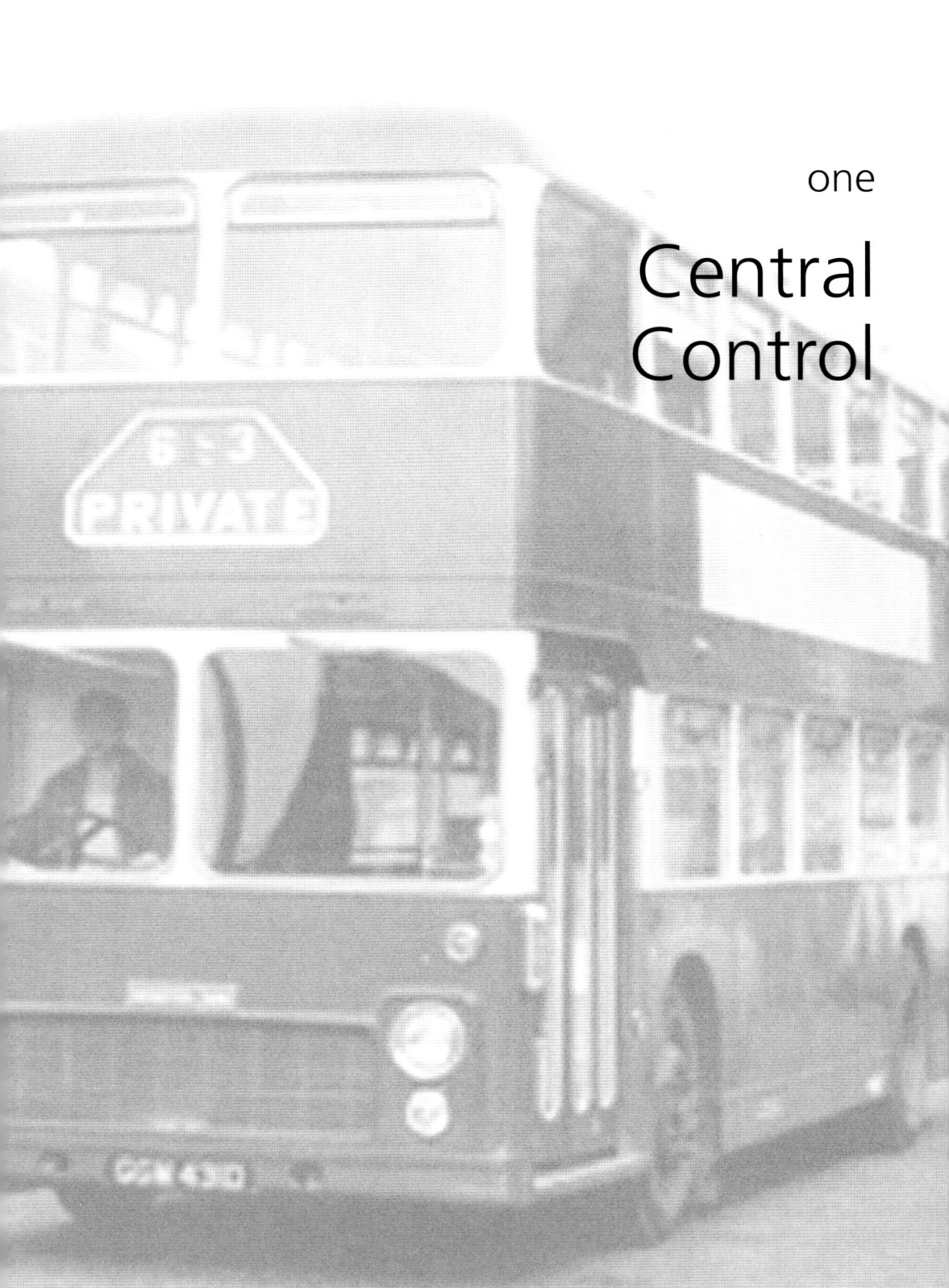

one

Central Control

The most familiar vehicles to be seen across Lanarkshire were undoubtedly those in the red and cream of Central SMT. Tracing its roots back to the Glasgow General Ominbus & Motor Services (GOC), the company changed its name in 1932.

Having already established routes throughout the county and acquired smaller operators in a rapid expansion, Central obtained control of the Lanarkshire Traction Company in August 1932. The latter continued as a separate subsidiary until 1949, the same year in which the nationalised British Transport Commission took over all bus interests of the Scottish Motor Traction Company (SMT), including Central.

With its HQ at Motherwell's Traction House, a former tramways depot of Lanarkshire Traction, Central's core network focussed on Hamilton, Motherwell and Wishaw, operating a somewhat complex but effective service system linking towns and villages with each other, and via its main trunk routes, with Glasgow (outwith the scope of this book is Central's Dunbartonshire operations).

Arguably due to the areas it covered and its more mundane bus operation, Central was perhaps the least 'glamorous' of the BTC's Scottish Bus Group companies. Astute management and operating policies, combined with controlled costs made Central one of the most consistently efficient companies in the BTC. Indeed, in consecutive years, 1957 and 1958 Central was 'top dog' with profits in excess of £1 million – a remarkable feat.

There's always a danger of wearing rose-coloured glasses when looking back, but a reddish hue in Central's case would surely be justified. Often maligned and berated by the public, as most transport operators have been at one time or another, Central did have its problems like other SBG companies, such as the occasional shortage of vehicles or industrial disputes. However, the overall level of performance was good. Regardless of the operator, the modern-day Lanarkshire bus passenger will find it impossible to make many A to B journeys, without changing at C, D or E. In some cases, service provision simply no longer exists.

Central's livery was basically red with cream relief for all buses, which was slightly modified for double-deckers in 1956. Coach deliveries from 1955 bore a new and attractive two-tone blue colour scheme.

The company's large fleet spread across Lanarkshire meant a number of depots: Motherwell/Hamilton/Wishaw/Carluke/East Kilbride plus Sub-depots at Harthill and Muirkirk. Today, only Motherwell (Airbles) survives as an operating centre for FirstBus, while Traction House is occupied by various retail and workshop traders.

Opposite below: Leyland had always been a favoured type, in many models and shapes over the decades. Whilst double-decks were more dominant, single-deck numbers were more than ample. This is the original T149 (the fleet class/number was repeated when applied to Leyland Leopards from the early 1960s to the early 1980s.) One of the final batch of PS1's with rear platforms dating from 1949, the Alexander-bodied vehicle wasn't withdrawn from Central service till 1964, when it passed to a building contractor for staff transport. T149 is in Hamilton Road, Motherwell, almost directly outside the front door of Central's HQ.

Above: Originally in the 'Lanarkshire' fleet, L220 was a 1935 Leyland TS7 which ran for Central until 1962. Its life span typified the company's standard of maintenance and operating use. Leaving Motherwell Depot yard, L220 is in the pre-1956 livery, hence the 'CENTRAL SMT CO LTD' legend which was painted in cerise on the cream waistband. (A.J. Douglas)

As late as 1954, Central ordered its final batch of rear-entrance, single-deckers, Guy Arab UFs, with forty-three-seat bus bodies by Walter Alexander. K49 is seen arriving in Carluke on Service 38 from Biggar. Following twelve years with Central, it saw further service with Shipbreaking Industries at Faslane. The location pictured here hasn't changed drastically, although the High Street shopping area has been pedestrianised. I often thought of these 'Coronation'-bodied 'K' types as 'Wise Guys', as the front looked like the face of a tawny owl! (A.J. Douglas)

Opposite above: When Bristol Commercial Vehicles produced their revolutionary 'Lodekka' (low height, double-decker), Central were quick to place orders. The company amassed 356 new Lodekkas in various guises between 1955 and 1967, making them the SBG's largest user of the type. As the fleet-number suggests, B2 was one of the initial batch with ECW H33/27R bodywork. The long radiator grille was indicative of early models. The location is Brandon Street, approaching Motherwell Cross, and B2 is destined for the town's Forgewood, a large housing estate on Service 41 from a similar locale, Pather, in Wishaw. This end of Brandon Street has long-since been transformed beyond recognition, replaced by a traffic-free, 'modern' shopping 'Parade'. The mobile butcher's van is from the maroon-liveried fleet of Dalziel Co-Operative, a well-known Lanarkshire institution which paid out its final dividend some years ago!

Opposite below: Pictured in Wishaw, B69 was from the 1957 batch of LD's, now with the shorter grille and standard SBG triangular destination layout. On its first repaint, this bus lost the cream surrounding the cab windows, and the fleet name between decks was shortened to 'Central'. (A.J. Douglas)

13

Between 1955 and 1960, the company shared its double-decker orders between Leyland and Bristol. L535 was a PD2/20 dating from 1956, carrying the 'squarer' Alexander L31/28R body. Part of Central's policy was to use new vehicles on its longer, trunk routes, and then later in their lives they'd be 'demoted' to shorter services. Changing crew at Hamilton L535 has travelled from Glasgow and is bound for Shotts, at that time a thriving, mining town on the eastern fringes of Lanarkshire.

New in 1960, L630 was Central's penultimate PD2/30 with the more stylish L31/28RD body by Alexander. Snapped in a more rural part of the county, the bus approaches Lesmahagow on the Limited Stop 51 Service from Glasgow (Killermont Street), on a journey lasting seventy minutes.

Further development of the Bristol Lodekka saw the FSF model introduced – FLAT floor, SHORT body, FRONT entrance. Central was the only SBG member to buy these new, seven in 1961, and a further forty-one over the following two years. B146, from the second batch, is seem climbing Quarry Street, in Hamilton, en route to the town's Northern suburb, Eddlewood. The shop proprietors have changed in this now-pedestrianised area. The names in shot here are evocative of the 1960s era – Grants' Furniture, Saxone Shoes, Hepworth's Tailors – as indeed are the parked cars, including Morris Minor, Hillman Minx and a Morris Oxford. The fizzy, soft drink 'Tizer' on the side-panel advert is still available – now made by Barr's. (A.J. Douglas)

In 1964, Central took delivery of thirty-five of the rear-entry FS model, fitted with manually-operated platform-doors. B200 is nearing its destination of West Calder, having crossed the Lanarkshire 'border' into West Lothian on an often-arduous cross-country trip from Strathaven. The scheduled journey time was two hours and forty-seven minutes! (A.J. Douglas)

Some years before one-man-operation became a reality, T6 is picking-up passengers on a Hamilton Local service. The location is again Hamilton's Quarry Street, just a few yards down the hill from the view on page 14. This vehicle was one of six Leyland Leopards with contemporary Alexander forty-one-seat bodywork delivered in 1961, before the 'invasion' over the next two decades of 400-plus Leopards with the stylish 'Y' type bodies. T6 was re-numbered TS6 when four years old, to distinguish them from the newer and bigger 'cats'! (R.F. Mack)

Central introduced another new marque into the fleet in 1962, when it purchased ten Albion Lowlander LR1 models, followed by a further twenty the following year. Despite their high-capacity seating (seventy-one), CSMT judged their performance to be poor, and in 1965 all were switched to other SBG companies, Highland and Alexander (Fife). (The same fate befell five Albion Viking rear-engined 'Y' type coaches in 1967, at less than two years into Central service.) A4 is laying-over at Strathaven before making the trip into Glasgow (Killermont Street). One of Lanarkshire's most picturesque towns, famous for its toffee and large public park, the Square has changed remarkably little, except the daily congestion by considerably more parked cars than shown here! (A.J. Douglas)

Chapter five looks at John Laurie's Chieftain operation, but when they sold out, Central inherited a fleet of thirty-one vehicles. Among the assortment were fifteen ex-London Transport RT's, which were given an 'H' prefix to distinguish them from the low-height fleet. HL 196 passes Traction House and two Central crew in old-style uniforms bearing some resemblance to Stan Butler and his conductor Jack in TV's *On The Buses*. The owner of the Ford Popular may have been eyeing-up the new Rover in Braedale Garage. A modern car showroom complex still occupies this site. (A.J. Douglas)

Two early-model Leyland Atlanteans came from Laurie, including the first from 1960. The SBG never really favoured the type, but HR 1 stayed with Central till 1969 when, along with its sister and two Leylands, it became the last ex-Chieftain vehicles to be withdrawn. HR 1 passed to Graham's of Paisley. It is shown here at an on-street terminus at Carlton Place on the south side of the River Clyde in Glasgow bound for Cambuslang. By the mid 1960s this end-point was abandoned in favour of the crowded and claustrophobic Waterloo Street.

Above and below: Central's priority was always bus operation, but the company did have coaches in the fleet for Private Hire work, as well as operating seasonal Day and Extended Tours. The most-favoured type was Bedford, two of which are pictured here. Above is C7, a 1955 SBG model with Duple thirty-eight-seat body, while below shows C21, which was one of a handful of SB5s bought new in 1963, with slightly larger forty-one-seat bodywork. Both vehicles saw further use by other Scottish independents after ten and six year's of Central service, respectively.

Opposite below: Central's highest capacity FLFs were the seventy-six (44/32) and seventy-eight (44/34) seaters, hence the 'BL' prefix ('Longest'). From the 1966 batch, BL312 arrives at Killermont Street to the north of Glasgow City Centre, in an area now occupied by Buchanan Bus Station, a multi-storey car park, and the Royal Concert Hall. The cigarette vending machine to the right of the bus is reminiscent of pre-health warning days on the dangers of smoking.

The reliability of the type kept Central loyal to the Lodekka right till the end of production, and beyond! Delivered new in 1965, BE 227 was a sixty-eight-seater which has been 'immortalised' in die-cast model form by EFE. The 'E' in the fleet number indicated 'extended' and applied to the sixty-eight and seventy-seat FLF's. The 240 from Glasgow to Lanark ran every fifteen minutes. Along with the 241 Carluke/Glasgow and the short-worked 40 to Motherwell or Wishaw, these services provided high frequency over arguably the main artery out of Lanarkshire. BE 227 is on Motherwell's Brandon Street after its first phase of modernisation but before it was closed to through traffic. The concrete-topped shop units stand where once the town's 'Wall' hid from view a large railway goods yard.

Above: When Bristol designed a new 'decker, the VRL, Central took one of their two prototypes on extended loan from 1966–1970. It became BN331 whilst in service, and was dubbed 'Big Nellie'. She's seen here on Low Waters Road climbing out of Hamilton. (A.J. Douglas)

20

Above: BE 360 came from the Thames Valley & Aldershot fleet as part of that Bristol Exchange. It's pictured in Wishaw garage, having worked the 44, another of the many services linking Lanarkshire with Glasgow. Note the modified fleetname, with a bolder 'Central' legend. The side-panel advert is appropriate – King's confectionery factory was just a short distance away from the depot, famous for their Mint Imperials and Oddfellows, which were aromatic-type sweets. (A.J. Douglas)

Left: After withdrawal, Central deployed some of its FLF's on Driver Training Duties. However, the last of the 1963 batch, BE 180, was converted into a uniform store, and re-numbered S51. It's shown here in 1981 promoting the Company's Day Tours, at a Fun Day in Strathclyde Park, less than a mile from Motherwell Depot. (D.G. MacDonald)

Opposite below: 'Big Nellie''s use led to orders from Central and other SBG members. 1969 saw the arrival of twenty Bristol VRTs, the standardised model with transverse engine. BN375 approaches Motherwell Cross from Merry Street on a local service. The soon-to-be-familiar black rectangular 'Pay As You Enter' (PAYE) sign above the grille signals the imminent era of One-Man-Operation (OMO). Poor performance and preference for the FLF saw all SBG companies swapping their VRT's in 1973 with National Bus Company (NBC) operators for late-model Lodekkas.

Central bought nineteen Leyland Leopards in 1964. After a three year gap, the bus-bodied 'Y' type was on the annual order books for almost the next decade-and-a-half. T86 from 1969 descends Wishaw's Kirk Road. Service 92 linked the town's Coltness area with Newarthill, a village just north east of Motherwell. Despite the end-points being less than six miles apart, the listed travel-time was forty minutes, due to the intentionally circuitous route. At the time of this view, around 1971, the service was still crew operated by these single-deckers. (R.F. Mack)

As the 1970s enfolded, the 'Y' underwent cosmetic surgery to the fifty-three-seat body. T 356 shows the 'newest' front. Note too the changed fleet name to 'Central Scottish'. This was part of the SBG's 1978 attempt at a more corporate identity among all its members, using a blue saltire, followed by 'Scottish' and preceded by the operating company's name. Leaving Hamilton Bus Station just after entering service, T 356 is on the cross-county 14 from the town's Meikle Earnock district to Coatbridge and was later extended to Monklands Hospital as its northern terminus. (A.J. Douglas)

Contrasting styles of a marque that was rare in the Central fleet – Daimler.

Above: D2 was one of a pair of CWG5's with wartime Brush fifty-five-seat bodies new in 1943. Captured in Glasgow towards the end of its working-life, D2 stayed in service till 1959 (A.E. Jones)

Below: Although eight further CWA6's followed in 1944, it was to be a remarkable twenty-seven years before CSMT bought it's next new Daimlers! The rear-engined 'Fleetline' model had been taken-up by SBG companies since the mid-1960s, mainly by Western and the Alexander group, and usually with Walter Alexander bodywork, but it wasn't till 1971 that Central followed suit. The company took delivery of thirty-five CRG6LX's, all with E.C.W. H43/34F bodywork but their Lanarkshire lives were extremely short – less than five years. Initially it appeared they'd suffer the same 'fate' as the Bristol VRT's and be part of an Anglo-Scottish swap-shop, but in the end the entire batch were transferred to other SBG companies in exchange for Leopards. D13 nears its destination at Motherwell's large council estate, Forgewood, on the 41, connecting the town with Burgh neighbour Wishaw. The illuminated 'Pay As You Enter' sign shows the service is one-man-operated in this mid-1970s shot. (A.J. Douglas)

A successful Scottish-Scandinavian partnership resulted in the front-engined Volvo Ailsa. The chassis/engines were built at the Irvine Truck & Bus factory of the Swedish manufacturer, and bodied by Walter Alexander at Falkirk. The model was named after the rocky island that sits off the Ayrshire Coast. Although pioneered and championed by SBG members Fife and Midland, it wasn't until 1978 that Central gave the marque its debut with ten Mark I's. The only highbridge double-deckers bought new by the company, CSMT gave them the 'AH' type code. Based at East Kilbride depot, AH2 is seen on the 77 into Glasgow (Buchanan Bus Station) from Hairmyres Hospital. (A.J. Douglas)

Opposite below: The SBG as a whole were slow to adopt the Leyland National, unlike their English counterparts in the NBC. In 1978, Central took delivery of a batch of twenty Mark I models and deployed them initially on Hamilton Local services worked by the town's Clydesdale (Bothwell Road) depot. N1 is seen shortly after transfer across the River Clyde to Wishaw, and ventures out of the garage on to service 44 into Glasgow, although the absence of a blind assumes the passengers know the destination from the number! (A.J. Douglas)

Although delivered just a year later, the Mark II Ailsas showed some differences to the earlier model, noticeably the higher driving position. This view taken at East Kilbride Town Centre Bus Station illustrates the contrast between AH2 and the newer AH11. Central's total purchase of the Ailsa was just thirty. (Gordon Stirling)

Central revised its livery in 1979 by applying more cream to some of its repaints and newer vehicles. Smart as it was, especially on the single-decks, the depots' drive-through washes must have been on overtime! N8 heads back to Airbles garage after finishing on the 90 at Greenhead Road in Wishaw. This view is taken in neighbouring Motherwell, at the top of Brandon Street. Chapman the Butchers is still in business, but not at this site. The Odeon cinema, just visible, has shown its last blockbuster movie, and is awaiting conversion to a Bingo Hall. The fine building has since stopped echoing to the cries of 'House!' or 'two fat ladies' and has been demolished. (M.B. Transport Photos)

Opposite above: Having acquired two Lancets with the takeover of Baillie Bros. way back in 1936, it was forty-two years before the Dennis name was seen again in the Central fleet. Between 1978 and 1983, the company accumulated no fewer than fifty-one new rear-engined Dominators, all with seventy-nine-seat bodywork by Alexander. The sole vehicle appropriate to the timescale of this book is D1, which was unique in having an 'AD' type body – the others had 'R' types. Pictured in Buchanan Street Bus Station, D1 was based at East Kilbride, apart from a short spell on SBG trials at Midland's Milngavie depot early in its life. Central re-allocated the 'D' code to this marque, previously prefixing the Daimler Fleetlines, but by this time all transferred to other SBG members. (Gordon Stirling)

In 1974, Alexander's introduced the 'T' type to their range of bodywork. Considerably different to the ubiquitous 'Y' type, with a squarer outline, stepped roofline, and deep windows, Central took only fifteen of these on Leopard chassis, all built in 1979 with dual-purpose forty-nine-seat bodies. (Gordon Stirling)

Before leaving Central SMT, a 'double flashback' to the first decade covered by this book – the 1950s, and two prime examples of the many pre-war vehicles still giving sterling service at that time.

Pictured in the Depot Yard at Motherwell, L96 was a 1937 all-Leyland TD4 whose life with Central lasted twenty-one years.

Picking-up in Hamilton in its latter days, L135 was a TD5 delivered new in 1939, and wasn't withdrawn till 1958. (A.J. Douglas)

two

Baxter's – A Broth of a Bus Company!

Mention the name 'Baxter's', and most people will automatically think of the independent, family-run canned soup and food manufacturer based in Fochabers, one of Moray's most scenic areas, in the north of Scotland. To transport aficionados and North Lanarkshire citizens of a certain age the same name conjures up memories of an independent bus operator, also family-founded and managed, who operated in two of the county's industrial adjoining towns, Airdrie and Coatbridge. However, unlike their nourishing namesakes, the bus company didn't resist take-over by a nationalised giant, and sadly, nor is it still in business today!

After starting out in haulage as early as 1914, James Baxter then began operating a regular bus service between Old Monkland, Coatbridge and Gartness, a small village south-east of Airdrie, a few years later. Working out of his yard in Southburn Road, Airdrie, he deployed small Leylands, Albions and Dennis vehicles, some of which had lorry and bus bodies to serve all of Mr Baxter's interests! Such was his enterprising spirit, he had 'demountable' bodies for carrying coal, general haulage, and of course passengers, all of which were interchangeable and switched using a lifting device and gantry. Within a decade he'd built up a network of services covering the Monklands area.

In 1934, he moved the company's base into premises just around the corner in Railway Road, Coatdyke, and five years later the operating name was changed to Baxter's Bus Service Ltd.

James Baxter's policy was to have a mixture of new and second-hand vehicles. Bought from Chesterfield Corporation, Baxter's No.4 was a Leyland TS6 with MCCW B32R body, new in 1934. It is seen in here West Canal Street, Coatbridge, shortly before withdrawal in the early 1950s. (A.E. Jones)

The post-war years saw the fleet grow in strength, and at its peak of some fifty-three vehicles, Baxter's B.S. was the largest independent operator in Scotland. Leyland was the favoured marque, along with AEC's and a few other 'exceptions'.

No.29 was one of three Roe-bodied Crossley DD42 'deckers bought new in 1948. Sold in 1960, this bus saw further service in Scotland with John Keenan of Coalhall in Ayrshire. Tram-lines are still to be seen, but with no overhead wires, this view in Coatbridge was taken post-1956, after Glasgow Corporation had stopped running the 'shooglies' into Monklands. To the rear of the bus is local landmark the Whitelaw Fountain, which has since been moved a mere few metres. The Airdrie Savings Bank building on the right is still in business.

By the mid 1950s, the combination of the size of the fleet and the prominence of more double-deckers saw the company look for larger premises. Baxter's acquired property in Airdrie's Gartlea Road, which had been Goldie's Victoria Engineering Works. They retained the original buildings, whose height could accommodate the height of 'deckers, refurbished a small office block at the front gate, and it became Victoria Garage. The success of such a well-run and indeed well liked bus operator drew increasing attention from the SBG, and in 1962, Baxter's succumbed and sold out to Scottish Omnibuses. It was agreed, the BBS name and staff would remain operational, but within months of takeover, SOL bosses decided to change the Baxter's fleet into the contemporary light green/cream livery of the Edinburgh company, with the 'Scottish' legend.

However, SOL hadn't reckoned on just how restless the local natives would be by this move. Some voted with their feet, and refused to travel on the green buses, as bookings for charters and Private Hires also fell, and such was the public feeling, SOL was forced into a U-turn. Not only were all the Victoria vehicles repainted back into Baxter's livery, but from that point on, any vehicle transferred from the main SOL fleet received the smart blue/ivory livery, as indeed did any new bus allocated to the Airdrie operation.

Significantly, the Baxter's name remained for fifteen years after the founder's son Robert had sold out to the SBG company, but the Queen's Silver Jubilee year of 1977 marked the end of over six decades of local bus service under that famous banner.

SOL, which itself changed its fleet name to Eastern Scottish back in the 1960s, eventually closed Victoria Garage, most of whose vehicles were transferred less than two miles up the road to ES's Clarkston Depot, on the eastern outskirts of Airdrie. For a few years, Monklands District Council used Victoria Garage fittingly as a Transport Depot, albeit for their Cleansing Dept, but it's now but a mere memory. The whole area was redeveloped, which culminated in the building of a Retail Park on the site.

Another Crossley double-decker from 1948, but CST 671 was bought second-hand by Baxter's in 1956 from Highland Transport. It gave four years service as No.32, and is pictured pulling away from the long line of corrugated bus-shelters on West Canal Street, Coatbridge. The three-storey building in the background is the Mines Rescue Station, whose services were invaluable during the coal-mining heydays. Even after the Lanarkshire pits had closed, the Station remained operational till practically the last lump of 'black gold' had been extracted from the surviving Scottish mines.

Picking up a substantial passenger-load on Coatbridge's Sunnyside Road, Baxter's No.3 was a Leyland PS1 with thirty-four-seat Brush bodywork. New to Yorkshire Woollen District (Fleet No.159), this single-decker was acquired by BBS in 1956, and was disposed of five years later to a showman. The destination displayed, 'Glenmavis' is a village to the north of both Coatbridge and Airdrie where Baxter's actually had a small 'sub-depot' used for the winter storage of coaches.

Parked-up in the yard at Victoria Garage, CVA 855 (No.37) strikes an impressive pose. New in 1947, this bus was one of a pair of AEC Regals with Duple C35F bodywork, and stayed in service till 1961, before passing to a contractor, along with sister vehicle CVA 854.

One of the most stylish coaches bought new by Baxter's was this Burlingham-bodied Bedford SB1 from 1959. Not only did No.49 survive the takeover by SOL in 1962, where it became C.21, but it was later transferred to Stark's, Dunbar, another once-famous independent whose identity was also retained by SOL after buy-out. TVD 649 is on a Private Hire in Glasgow's Union Street, recognisable by the Ca'd'Oro building, which was ravaged by fire in recent times.

Navigating the roundabout at Coatbridge's Blair/Townhead/Gartsherrie/Lomond Roads junction is HVD 60 (No.55), an all-Leyland PD2 bought new by Baxter in 1953. The Townhead suburb of Coatbridge which itself expanded after the Second World War, was well served by Baxter's. Some routes ran via Townhead Road, others via Lomond Road, as shown here, and terminated at three different points in the 'scheme' – Wilton St, Lomond Road and 'The 30mph sign' (at the extreme west end)! The gap-site on the corner was soon to be filled by a pub, less-than- imaginatively named 'La Ronde'. HVD 60 became HH25 and stayed in service till June 1968. After takeover, Baxter's fleet number was carried in tandem with the SOL number, until the vehicle was taken off Baxter's routes. In March 1967, Baxter's numbers again became the 'official' fleet listing, but from the same month in 1971, only SOL numbers were used. (A.J. Douglas)

Opposite below: Baxter's livery on single-decks was two shades of blue with ivory relief. The roof had the 'normal' dark blue, and the body a lighter hue. On later repaints some singles had the darker shade applied to their bottom 'skirts'. NVA 142 (106/B17) was another AEC Reliance with 1956 contemporary Alexander B45F body. The location is Coatbridge Main Street. The buildings on the right still stand, all occupied by totally different traders, while those on the left have were replaced by modern shop 'blocks' in the 1970s. (A.J. Douglas)

Above: Baxter's 103 was exhibited at the 1954 Earl's Court Motor Show. It was a forty-four-seat AEC Reliance with Crossley body. Numbered B12 by SOL, KVA 750, shown here at the Fountain crossover in Coatbridge, ended its days with Crudens, the Musselburgh contractor, after being withdrawn in 1969.

Two examples of what made the Monklands people see red! The burghers of Coatbridge and Airdrie were far from amused by SOL's decision to convert their beloved blue Baxter's fleet into the SBG company's green/cream colours, but as noted above the protests were successful and the policy reversed.

Above: Pictured laying-over at Clarkston in the short-lived livery is Baxter's 107 (H2), an all-Leyland PSU1 new in 1952. Baxter's purchased this bus from Corless & Son of Coppull when it was five years old and it was a decade later before it was withdrawn, ending its days as a mobile canteen with West Lothian Council Roads Dept.

Below: Even the large 'B' in the destination display had been blanked out on Baxter 59 (HH29) in the SOL makeover. FVD 224 and sister bus FVD 225 (pictured on p.2) came to Baxter's second-hand from Irvine of Salsburgh, whose operations are featured in Chapter nine. PD2 was stripped for spares in December 1968. (Both pics. A.J. Douglas)

From the mid-1950s till the SOL take-over, Baxter's bought a total of eighteen new Leyland double-deckers with bodywork by Massey Bros. Shown in its latter days, 61 (HH31), from 1956, has just past Broomfield Park, the former home of Airdrieonians F.C. A supermarket now occupies the site of the famous old ground, unique and distinguished by its pavilion, seen on the left.

The Wigan manufacturer also supplied similar style bodies on two AEC Regent V chassis in 1957. No.68 (BB20) is caught by the camera heading towards Sikeside in Coatbridge, despite the destination screen, which appears to have been prematurely changed for the return trip to the town's Kirkshaws area. Along with 67 (BB19), this vehicle was transferred into the main Eastern Scottish fleet, and at the age of seventeen in 1974, the pair saw further brief service with Alexander (Northern).

These two photographs of Baxter 70 (HH 38) show off the stylish lines of the Masssey bodies. TVA 70 was new in 1957 and was withdrawn after sixteen year's service, and sold off to Locke, the Edinburgh dealer who took most of SOL's disposals.

Above: The detailed destination display was typical of Baxter's operation. The company didn't use service numbers, hence the blacked out box on the right. Only in the twilight years of SOL/Eastern Scottish rule, were numbers in the 29-range utilised. In this view on Airdrie's Graham Street, 70 is followed by an SOL Lodekka from Clarkston depot on a trunk service to Glasgow. (S.J. Kelly)

Below: Baxter's roundel, with name and telephone number is seen clearly as TVA 70 and a sister vehicle turn from West Canal Street into Bank Street on a wet day in Coatbridge. The building to the right of the rail bridge is still there, not as the Fountain Cafe, but as the control office for a local taxi firm. (A.J. Douglas)

Baxter's 111 became B22 on takeover. New in 1958, the Burlingham-bodied AEC Reliance spent its whole fifteen-year life on local services and is heading down Airdrie's Graham Street, a once-busy thoroughfare now inevitably pedestrianised. The ecclesiastical looking building overshadowing the bus was the former Caledonian Railway station, closed to passengers in 1943, but retained as a Goods Depot long after, before demolition in the early 1960s.

Picking-up at the stop designated only for Coatbridge services, 118 (B29) is also on the same street. Woolworth's store is still in situ today, but the buildings to the rear of the car have been replaced. New in 1960 with contemporary Alexander B45F body, 118 passed to Twell, the dealer of Ingham, in 1975. The destination shown, 'Gartsherrie', was once the location of the famous Baird's iron and steel works, now long gone and the majority of the site taken up by a 'Freightliner' Terminal and Container base.

Of all the Massey-bodied 'deckers, four delivered in 1960/61 were the most interesting and 'handsome' vehicles. Baxter's 74-77 (HH42-45) had one-piece sliding-door front entrances. These were built to Baxter's specifications after long discussions on design with the bodybuilder and they were unique apart from a few taken by Birkenhead's municipal fleet. 74 is still fairly new in this shot, taken on Main Street/Deedes Street, Coatdyke. The latticed girder bridge carries the main Airdrie-Helensburgh/Balloch North Electric rail lines, while the gap site to its left was 'filled in' by 1960s blocks of three-storey flats. The building on the immediate left of the bus now houses a launderette. (A.J. Douglas)

Baxter's 78 was one of what should have been three-of-a-kind – AEC Bridgemasters with Park Royal seventy-three-seat bodies. Although ordered by the company, what would have been 79 was diverted to Red Rover of Aylesbury. No.80 was actually finished in Baxter's colours and registered 480 DVA, but it entered service directly with SOL as BB 962 (9962 SF). New in December 1961, 78 (BB18) was exhibited at that year's Scottish Motor Show. Shortly after acquiring Baxter's business, SOL transferred this bus into the main fleet, and it saw further SBG service with Highland from 1973. (A.J. Douglas)

As with the Bridgemasters, 9961 SF had been ordered by Baxter for 1963, but by then SOL had kicked-in, and the modern Daimler CRG with Alexander H40/33F entered service in the parent company's colours. However, within a year, the bus was converted into Baxter's livery, becoming No.79 at Victoria Garage. The crew pose for the photographer on Bank Street, Coatbridge.

In 1965, 79 was badly damaged by fire. Eventually it was rebodied and returned to service, but initially No.80 (DD80) was drafted in as a replacement in July of that year. It had been destined for Western SMT as their 2012, but was diverted to Baxter's. The Morris 1100 saloon threatens to contradict the advert on the side-panel of 80, parked at the Kirkwood end-point in Coatbridge. Both Daimler Fleetlines moved into the Eastern Scottish fleet at the end of the Baxter's era.

The penultimate new delivery to Baxter as a true independent was 42 (B32), a 1962 AEC Reliance with forty-one seats on a Plaxton coach body. In 1965,'Z' was added to the SOL fleet number, indicating dual-purpose use. Tagged with the simplified Baxter '42V' moniker, 42 CVD sits at Airdrie Cross on stage-service to Old Monkland, Coatbridge. (S.Kelly)

Only weeks after the take-over, the movement of buses from the SOL fleet into the Baxter ranks began. AA 891 (along with 892/3/4) all became blue Bristol FLF's from 1962 based at Victoria as Nos 91-94. The first of the foursome is at the eastern end of Coatbridge's Main Street. The 'wasteland' to the left, and buildings to the vehicle's rear are now totally transformed to include a restaurant/grill/hotel complex called 'Centre Point'.

In 1967, several five-year-old AEC Reliances were transferred to the Baxter series. B902V is destined for Carnbroe a former mining village but now home to numerous private housing estates, just south of Coatbridge. Just visible on the nearside windscreen is the 'economy' OMO sign – 'Please Pay As You Enter'. This vehicle was scrapped at Dunsmore's Larkhall yard in 1978.

As more and more of original Baxter's vehicles 'reached their own terminus', the Edinburgh overlords re-inforced the Airdrie fleet accordingly. B923V arrived at Victoria at the same time as the vehicle above, but being a year younger, it carried Walter Alexander's then new 'Y' type body. This was a 'short' version, favoured by SOL, who also took the longer models on both bus and coach bodywork. Pictured turning on to West Canal Street, 923 (later to be ZB classed) is on an all-Coatbridge service linking Townhead, Wilton Street with Renfrew Street, Kirkwood. Although these council schemes virtually sat on either side of the main A89 trunk road out of Coatbridge, the route ran via the Town Centre, as many did, to give both communities frequent access. Barnsley dealer P.V.S. took this bus and many of her 'sisters' following their withdrawal in the late summer of 1978. (A.J. Douglas)

Although Bristol FLFs could be seen in Baxter's colours relatively quickly after SOL's buy-out, it was several more years before open platform Lodekkas (LDs) 'graced' the local livery. AA 583/4 switched to Victoria Garage in 1970. New to SOL in 1957, this pair finished service in 1973. With a further three-year stay-of-execution for 583 as a driver-trainer, both befell the same ultimate fate – the breakers' blowtorch.

Above: Carrying a contemporary SBG advertising slogan, AA 583 is seen on West Canal Street in the days before the area was flattened for modernisation. The female passenger waiting to alight holds a 'trendy' shopping basket with nylon cover! The 'Mills' on the lower rear advertisement panel was a long-established Lanarkshire family TV and audio business, now permanently 'switched off'! (A.J. Douglas)

Below: AA 584 displays the modified destination display within the customary SBG 'triangle', with route numbers now being used. Like its Airdrie counterpart, the Woolworth store still remains, but the adjacent John Temple Tailor has long since measured their last inside-leg. Now closed to through traffic, this section of Coatbridge Main Street is still a busy area. (A.J. Douglas)

ZB160 was half of a pair of AEC Reliances delivered new in two-tone blue and grey in 1966, with Alexander 'Y' C49F bodies. Numbered 160/161 in the Baxter series, EWS 160D is being manoeuvred by a mechanic in the depot yard. The chrome bumper 'disappeared' at a later date.

Like its SBG colleagues, Eastern Scottish/SOL indulged in the great 'VRs for FLFs' swap-shop in 1973. AA 995 came from the United Automobile fleet, Darlington, where it had been their 548 and bought new in 1968. Stationery in this snapshot in Coatbridge, 995 is being overtaken by one of Baxter's 'own' front-entrance PD2s.

As already noted, SOL continued to supply new vehicles in Baxter colours till two years before they terminated the operation. ZH 476 was one of two Leyland Leopards delivered in 1973. It is approaching Coatbridge Town Centre en route to Glenmavis, and has obviously suffered accident damage to its front, near-side. (MB Transport Photographs)

The final bus delivered new in the famous colours was DD 694, one of a trio of 1975 Daimler Fleetlines with ECW seventy-five-seat bodywork. The first phase of town-centre redevelopment in Coatbridge has taken place – the building on the left is the Asda Superstore. While 694 is about to set-down passengers at the stops on the South Circular Road, the supermarket's car park holds an interesting assortment of vehicles. (A.J. Douglas)

three

Hutchie's Hold Over Towns

The village of Overtown sits on the North side of the River Clyde, but virtually overlooking the Clyde Valley. Once a thriving mining community with its own colliery, Overtown has a significant place in the history of Lanarkshire's transport, thanks to one of its own 'sons'.

Isaac Hutchison started a bus service in 1919 between Wishaw and his home village, and later extended across the valley to Larkhall. He was a formative part of a bold initiative seven years later in the Lanarkshire A1 Bus Operators' Association, which saw several independents working in partnership to compete against the Glasgow General Company (GOC) on the Newmains to Glasgow route. Hutchison left the A1 group, a short-lived co-operative, to concentrate on his own local services, which he did to great effect.

Not only did his blue buses become familiar sights, but Isaac had the foresight to provide miners' services, linking many of the 'pits' in the county's coalfield. Private Hire and Tour work was also developed. As motorised transport in general became more common, his enterprise saw him open a filling station on Overtown Main Street, on a site still occupied by such a facility to this day. He also owned a fruit orchard, but bus operation was the main business.

In the early days, Hutchison, like other operators, patronised Scottish manufacturer Albion, but moved on to others, like Leyland. The fleet grew via a combination of new and second-hand purchases, and although dominated by single-decks, Hutchison did deploy 'deckers, the first bought in 1938.

The death of Isaac Hutchison in 1960 was followed by the formation of a new company, Hutchison's Coaches (Overtown) Ltd., headed by Sam Anderson, a road-haulier of some renown from nearby Newhouse. The incorporation was helped by Ernest Sanderson of Glasgow dealer Millburn Motors, whom Hutchison regularly used for buying/selling vehicles. Originally secretary, Isabella Irvine, Mr Anderson's wife (whose family's bus operations are featured elsewhere in this volume), became a director in 1963.

The declining mining industry led to 'Hutchies', as they are affectionately known, extending into Motherwell and starting up new routes, both within Wishaw and down to its burgh partner. It was the introduction of service No.4 between Coltness (Wishaw) and Forgewood (Motherwell) which sparked a somewhat unusual battle with the 'big boys' of Central SMT. The nationalised operator complained that Hutchison's service, run on a frequency of three buses an hour, was taking traffic away from their own routes which connected and ran through the two towns. After re-applying, Hutchisons were granted a short-term licence, but Central won a successful objection to the fresh application. The stand-off between the two operators forced the local Burgh Councillors to lobby the Minister of Transport at the time, Barbara Castle. She duly decreed the rival companies had to compromise and supply co-ordinated services within the area. Consequently, the independent had to fine-tune their network with Central basically filling timetable gaps between Motherwell and Wishaw.

The co-operation may not have been done in perfect harmony, but the tale has a bizarre twist, with SBG interest becoming more substantial. In the late summer of 1967, the smaller operator was renamed Anderson (Tippers) Ltd., a motorbus and coach hirer, while a 'new' Hutchison's Coaches (Overtown) Ltd. was formed. The directors of this latter company were all SBG staff, but the daily running and responsibility remained with the Anderson family – the waters were certainly muddied. The locals, however, saw no change to their 'Hutchie buses', and remarkably, after three years, the SBG-financed company 'vanished', and the true independent status was regained. The 'tipper' company reverted to its original name.

From the 1960s, the company policy was to buy mainly new vehicles, with the AEC Reliance, on both bus and coach chassis, becoming the mainstay of a fleet whose strength peaked at the forty mark in the period relevant to this book.

Parked-up in Hutchison's original yard in Overtown is this Albion Valkyrie with Duple coachwork. It was bought second-hand from Carlisle-based Blair & Palmer. The elaborate crest with the company name was phased out by the early 1960s. (A.J. Douglas)

Another Duple-bodied Albion, this time a Victor, is pictured on a street in Overtown. The Austin van, probably a mobile shop, is typical of the period. The style of council housing, built between the wars, could be found in many Lanarkshire towns and villages. (A.J. Douglas)

Compared to their single-deck counterparts, double-deck buses were always in the minority. The Glasgow registration plate on this Daimler and its sister vehicle behind may suggest they were ex-Glasgow Corporation, but in fact they'd come from an independent, Northern Roadways. This pair had bodywork by Barnard of East Anglia. (A.J. Douglas)

Climbing out of the Clyde Valley is RVA 763, an N.C.M.E.-bodied Leyland PD2. The Larkhall/Wishaw route was a 'cross-river' service and involved steep inclines on both sides of the famous waterway. Hutchison stopped operating 'deckers in 1965. (A.J. Douglas)

An evocative scene from the late 1950s as workers board a Bedford C5 with Duple bodywork. The location is Castlehill Road in Overtown. Hutchie's Depot now occupies this site which at that time was only an open yard. The winding-gear of the small local colliery can be seen in the background.

Taken at the same spot, this view shows another C5, but with a shorter thirty-seat body. This bus, similar to those supplied to MacBrayne's, stayed in service till 1965. The conductress posing for the camera is wearing an overall, as Hutchison didn't use 'bespoke' uniforms as such. (A.J. Douglas)

Before the company 'standardised' on AEC's, Hutchison occasionally had the odd 'curiosity' in the fleet. This little bus was a Commer-Beadle Integral, and later passed to Wilson, Carnwath. (A.J. Douglas)

Leaving Larkhall for Wishaw, KVA 511 was actually the last double-decker to operate in service. A 1954 all-Leyland Titan PD2, this bus was sold on to Stonier, of Stoke-on-Trent. (A.J. Douglas)

A puddled car park somewhere in the Highlands is the setting for this Albion Victor with Duple Firefly coachwork. The whole trio of such vehicles bought new in 1963, were traded to SMT Sales & Service just three years later. (A.J. Douglas)

A quick glance and you might think this is a MacBrayne's vehicle in some scenic part of the Western Highlands. It is, of course, a Hutchie's coach travelling through a rural part of its home county. The scarf fluttering out of the rear window of this 1961 Duple Donnington-bodied AEC Reliance hints it may be on a football/rugby supporters' charter. (A.J. Douglas)

Taking day-trippers to the Ayrshire coast, YVD 179 was a Ford Thames coach with Duple Yeoman forty-one-seat bodywork. After eight years in the blues and cream of Hutchison, this vehicle retained its 'uniform' when bought by a Boys Brigade Company in Baillieston on the Lanarkshire/Glasgow border. Like several other battalions who also made similar contemporary purchases from other operators, this vehicle was in 'Sure and Steadfast' condition. (A.J. Douglas)

The sloping driver's windscreen typifies the Willowbrook bus short body on this AEC Reliance. 719 AVA was unusual in not having a numbers aperture in its display. Also snapped on a Private Hire into Ayrshire, this bus saw further service there from 1966 with Paterson of Dalry. (A.J. Douglas)

The use of paper destination labels by Central and other SBG companies was often criticised, but Hutchison's occasionally had to resort to this practice. In this instance it would appear to be justified in this 1970 view. Service 2 from Overtown had just been extended from Wishawhill to Motherwell Cross, and journeyed 'down the hill' via Craigneuk. The company was the first Scottish independent to introduce service numbers, in 1964. The bus is a 1965 Reliance, while the billboards are of note – Cigarette adverts are now banned, while the *Motherwell Times* continues to appear in the area on a weekly basis.

One of a batch of 36ft-long Reliances, also bodied by Willowbrook, DVA 166C, has just crossed the Garrion Bridge, before climbing up into Larkhall. Decades of congestion and accidents at this Clyde crossing, has recently seen the construction of a second bridge across the river to carry the southbound flow (from Wishaw to Clyde Valley, Larkhall and beyond). (A.J. Douglas)

When ordered to co-ordinate and co-operate with Central in 1967, Hutchie's 'tweaked' their 1 and 4 routes, and also introduced Service 5. This half-hourly running linked Coltness with Forgewood, taking twenty-eight minutes to complete the journey. From a trio of Reliances delivered new that year, KVD 14E approaches Motherwell Cross on Merry Street.

Walter Alexander produced the 'W' body in 1968, and Hutchison's took four AEC Swifts to this specification. The location is Motherwell's Brandon Parade after the first phase of town centre redevelopment, when still open to through-traffic. Along with its 'sisters', this bus was transferred to Dundee Corporation's municipal fleet in 1970.

Bedfords did get the occasional 'nod of approval', as shown by this Plaxton bodied coach bought in 1970. (A.J. Douglas)

Changes to Hutchison's livery in the time span of this book were fairly minor and 'cosmetic', until the early 1970s. The company experimented with this bus as a 'guinea-pig', wearing a dark blue skirt, cream covering the greater area and a light blue centre band and roof. Six Reliances delivered in 1970/71were split between fifty-five-seat bus bodies and fifty-one-seat dual-purpose configuration, all by Plaxton. YVA 143J fell into the latter category, and is pictured in Wishaw turning from Main Street into Caledonian Road. The Horse Shoe Bar is still a well-patronised watering-hole, but now as the trendier 'Centre Point'. (A.J. Douglas)

The livery was fully revamped when the dark blue was dropped altogether, leaving an all-over light blue with cream relief, as modelled here on this 1971 Willowbrook-bodied Reliance. Note the appearance of the large 'H' which was to become an on-going feature, and the display of fleet numbers. This bus was No.49 and is seen on Wishaw Main Street bound for Larkhall. (A.J. Douglas)

Above: A 'one-off' colour scheme was applied to Hutchison's 'one-off' vehicle. This 1973 Leyland National was bought new, and was painted blue with white roof and bumper. Within a couple of years, it had made the short journey up the road to Law Village, where it joined the fleet of Irvine's.

Opposite middle: It appears the crew on this 1975 Reliance are relying on their passengers' route knowledge by only displaying a number 4. The route was Coltness to Forgewood. This bus is passing a Central Leopard, as it pulls away from the row of bus stops on West Hamilton Street in Motherwell. The academic building was a school for generations, latterly as an annexe for Dalziel H.S., but is now the Dalziel Workspace and Training Centre. (A.J. Douglas)

Opposite below: New in 1976, this bus was delivered with the familiar rectangular 'Pay As You Enter' sign already fitted, but due to service frequencies and demands, Hutchie's did not introduce OMO till into the 1980s. Pictured on Wishaw's Stewarton Street, the 'Young Trend' Babywear and Children's Wear shop is still in business, but today's customers are the 'youngsters' of the 1970s buying for their own offspring, or even grandchildren! (A.J. Douglas)

Left: Despite the confusing blind, FVA 486K heads down Motherwell's Airbles Road on a rather crowded private hire. Although it was a Willowbrook fifty-one-seat coach body, this Reliance had two-leaf folding doors and destination screen. All of the cars in shot are Fords, which is perhaps not too surprising. There's been a large dealership in the town for decades, since Ian Skelly's 'Skellyford' days through to the current Reg Vardy outlet. (A.J. Douglas)

Above: On the outskirts of Larkhall after its cross-Clyde journey from Wishaw, UGB 13R was from a trio of 1977 Reliances with Duple bus bodywork. (A.J. Douglas)

Right: The No.3 service was extended in the mid-1960s to terminate at Motherwell's Strathclyde Hospital. Captured in summer sunshine at Wishaw Cross, JGE 347T was part of the company's 1979 intake.

Below: NGD 20V marked the end of Hutchison's AEC era, being their last Reliance, before the company standardised on the Volvo B58.

Although this image brings the chapter to a close, the route on which it is shown is rather symbolic. Service 6, a Wishaw 'Local Rover' service, linking Coltness with Netherton (Carbarns) was only introduced, when 20V was new in 1980. Hutchison's are still to the fore in the twenty-first century. In an era of new operators and competition, the company, still under the ownership of the Anderson family, continues to provide reliable stage-carriage services with a smart, and well-maintained fleet of vehicles, and of course, Private Hire and extended tours.

four
Carmichael's 'Highland' Fling

To be recognised in transport circles is one thing, but to be hailed a war hero and hold a place in Scotland's military history easily surpasses the status of a mere bus operator. John Carmichael from Glenmavis, by Airdrie, was serving as a Sergeant in the 9th Staffordshire Regiment during the First World War. In 1917, the NCO was digging trenches in Zwarteleen, Belgium, when a live grenade landed. The twenty-four-year-old Carmichael saved the lives of his men by telling them to clear the trench and he covered the missile with his helmet and foot. The explosion caused John to suffer severe injuries, and he spent the remainder of the conflict in a Liverpool hospital. His gallantry was duly recognised when King George V presented John Carmichael with the Victoria Cross medal at Buckingham Palace. He is one of fourteen Lanarkshire men to have received such a decoration.

Carmichael's bravery wasn't lost on his local community, and the people of Airdrie gave him money, which he used to buy a chicken farm in New Monkland. After purchasing a further two such poultry establishments, John then diversified totally and started a bus service from his base at the Meadows in Glenmavis. His main route linked Kilsyth with Coatbridge, and served a host of mining communities. He also commenced operations into Glasgow and then from the city to Helensburgh on the Clyde Coast. By 1931 John had moved to Helensburgh and had intended to further develop services into the West Highlands, hence the reason he used the fleet name 'West Highland Bus Service', but the 'West' was dropped at an early stage.

In 1932, his Glasgow to Helensburgh run, along with local services in Dunbartonshire, were acquired by Central SMT, and twelve months later W. Alexander took the Glasgow-Annathill route. John relocated to Glenboig, a nearby village to Glenmavis, and focussed on operating services from Coatbridge to Kilsyth and Annathill, in addition to Private Hire work for his coaches.

During the Second World War, John Carmichael was still determined to serve his country, and he enlisted as a Lieutenant in the 2nd Lanarkshire Btn of the Home Guard in 1942, whilst continuing to operate his business. 'Highland' livery was always red, latterly with cream relief. In the early days, the vehicles carried tartan waistbands, an embellishment which was commonly favoured by other operators of the day. John Carmichael was also fiercely loyal to the all-Scottish Albion marque, not necessarily out of sentimentalism, but because of their reliability and durability. In the twilight years of business, he began to standardise on Leylands.

When the 'New Town' of Cumbernauld was evolving in the mid-1960s, Carmichael challenged Alexander (Midland) over the provision of services. He succeeded in being granted licences for all internal town services, plus one through service to Kilsyth, while the SBG company won the other through-routes. However, attempts to extend the Coatbridge-terminating services into Airdrie were thwarted by natural opposition from Baxter's and Scottish Omnibuses.

In the summer of 1966, John Carmichael agreed to sell-out to Alexander (Midland), who took over all the remaining vehicles and services but only used the yard until their own brand-new depot in Cumbernauld, was built and opened the following year. After a decade of retirement, John Carmichael, V.C., died in 1977 at the age of eighty-four and he was buried with full military honours in New Monkland Cemetery, in his native Glenmavis.

Opposite below: As Highland's No.19, CCX 880 was one of a quartet of ex-Hansons of Huddersfield vehicles. New in 1945, Carmichael purchased this bus in 1949 and had it rebuilt to B35F by Pickering in 1960. The other three former Hansons' Valkyries didn't arrive at Glenboig till 1950/1, via Uniline Coaches of Preston. CCX 880 also had a long life and it even passed into Alexander's Midland fleet on takeover as MNA 1, but was withdrawn and disposed of in January 1967.

Above: The Highland fleet was always an eclectic mix of new and second-hand vehicles. The former is represented here, as Carmichael's No.16 turns into Water Street in Coatbridge. This was an Albion Valkyrie with thirty-five-seat bus body by Pickering of Wishaw. Bought new in 1946, it gave an incredible nineteen years service. The church on the hill, formerly Gartsherrie Parish, is still extant, but is now St Andrews. The three-windowed building above the rear of the bus was a bank at the time of this picture, but is now a bookmakers. (A.J. Douglas)

With thirty-three-seat Duple coach body from 1948, SB 6908 was sold to Highland nine years later by Fitzpatrick of Dunoon. It too passed to Midland, as MNA 2 and was withdrawn along with MNA 1. (J.G. Nye)

Carmichael did operate double-deckers, but only a few. Parked up in the Greenfoot Garage yard is BCS 343, a 1947 all-Leyland PD1 with L27/26R bodywork. It came second-hand from Western SMT in 1965, where it had been their 493. Midland also acquired this vehicle re-classed MRA 58, but it had been withdrawn within six months. In this view, it is flanked by HAT 645, an ex-East Yorkshire Leyland Tiger of 1947 vintage, and just in shot on the right FYS---, one of six Royal Tigers bought from Glasgow Corporation.

Opposite above: One of three ex-Ribble Leyland PD2/3s, DRN 281 joined the Highland fleet in 1964, and actually stayed in service with Midland as MRB 282 till 1969. John Carmichael stayed in Greenfoot Cottage adjunct to the yard, and near the main rail line. The house today is still occupied by an elderly relation of his. (J.G. Nye)

Opposite middle: Another former Ribble 'decker (their 2505) in Carmichael's fleet approaches Coatbridge Fountain westbound on Main Street. Bought when eleven years old, in 1958, this Brush-bodied Leyland PD1 worked hard for Highland till 1965. These buildings are long-gone, replaced by modern shop units, and the only trader of those in shot, still doing business is Boots. (Photobus)

Right: Carmichael's allegiance to Albion was commendable, but as already mentioned their long-lasting vehicles made economic sense. FVA 650 was a Valiant coach with Duple body bought new in 1950. Although it became their MNA 5, Midland disposed of this vehicle in January 1967, and it was broken-up by a Glasgow 'scrappie', along with some of its 'sisters' in the same class.

Right: Scottish Aviation supplied the thirty-five-seat bus body on this 1950 Albion Valkyrie. Despite open parking, Carmichael's policy of good care and maintenance helped see this vehicle also passing to Midland as MNA 4.

Above: With thirty-three-seat coachwork by Burlingham, this Leyland PS1 was thirteen years old when it passed to Highland in 1961 from Standerwick of Blackpool, where it had been their No.105. It gave its new owner four years service. (R. Marshall)

Opposite above: New in 1951, Carmichael built the body on this Albion Valiant. Although just returned from schools duty in this photograph, GVA 324 survived to pass into the Midland fleet as MNA 7 but only to exist another few short months. (J.G. Nye)

Opposite middle: Between 1965/66, Highland took in six Leyland Royal Tiger Worldmasters from Glasgow Corporation. These all had forty-four-seat bodies built by G.C.T. to Weymann design. New in 1957, FYS 692 had been LS/21 in the 'Corpy' fleet, and became MPF 3 after Midland's takeover, and stayed active till 1971. Note the tartan band between the headlamps – a throwback to Carmichael's earlier days. (J.G. Nye)

Opposite below: Some vehicles arrived at Glenboig via a circuitous route – DEK 41 was new to Smith, Wigan, in 1957. It came north to Robert Duncan of Motherwell, before passing to Mitchell of Glasgow who sold the Albion Aberdonian to Highland in 1964. It has a Plaxton forty-one-seat coach body, and survived with Alexander till 1972 as MNL/19, alongside MNL/20 (OVD 947), a sister Aberdonian bought new by Carmichael.

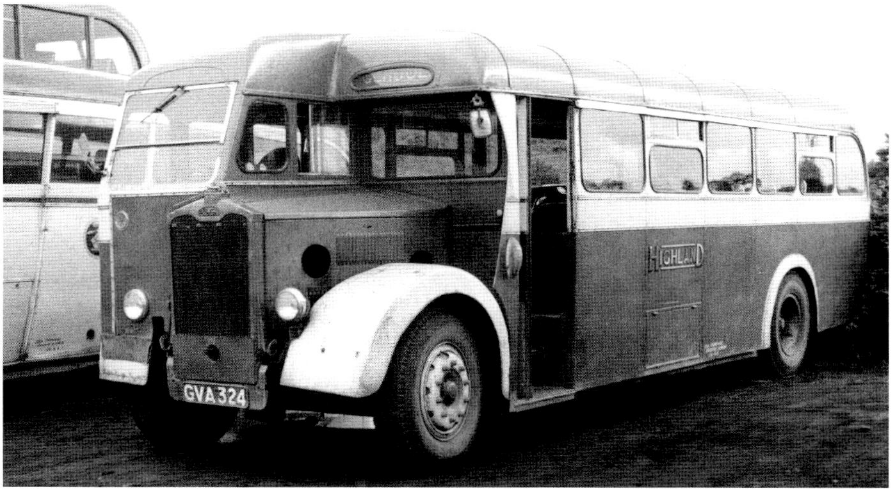
HIGHLAND
GVA 324

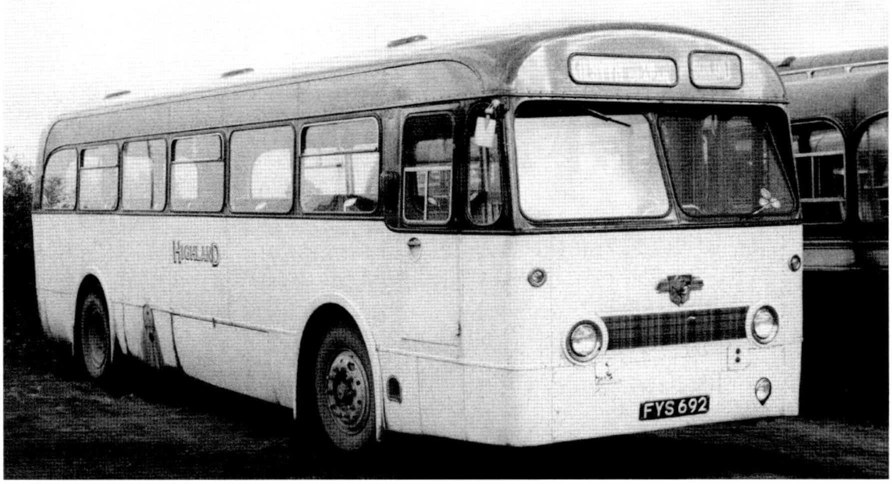
HIGHLAND
FYS 692

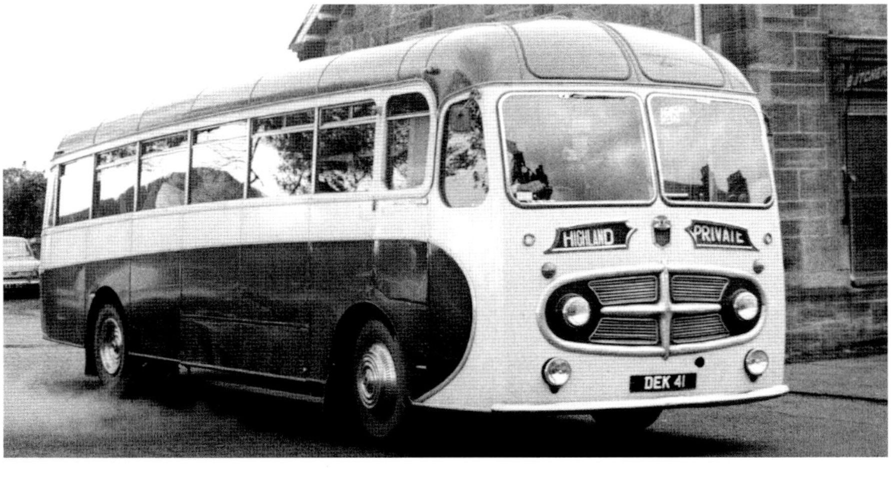
HIGHLAND
PRIVATE
DEK 41

Top: Highland's 'terminus' in Coatbridge was not in the town centre, but a piece of industrial wasteland on the banks of the Monkland Canal, across the main A89 road from Albion Rovers FC's Cliftonhill stadium. This area has been completely transformed, and is now occupied by a supermarket, car park, office block, and Ford dealership. Laying-over on the old site is 764 BVA, one half of a pair of Leyland Leopards with contemporary Alexander forty-five-seat bodywork purchased new in 1961. The only other Leopards with this style of body were a batch of six L2's supplied to Central SMT (see Chapter one). The two Highland Leopards slipped 'unnoticed' into the Midland pack as MPE 83/84, and lasted till 1971. (A.J. Douglas)

Middle: When John Carmichael won the licence for Cumbernauld Town Services, he ordered this Leyland PD2/3 in 1962. It had H41/31F bodywork by Alexander to the same specification as Glasgow Corporation buses of similar make, and was the only 'decker ever bought new. Pictured at North Carbrain, this vehicle stayed in the New Town after takeover, as did many Carmichael acquisitions, at Midland's Cumbernauld depot. As their MRB 282 it lasted till the spring of 1974.

Bottom: The penultimate vehicle bought new by Highland was 610 GVD, a 1963 Leyland Leopard with Willowbrook forty-five-seat body. It is seen here leaving West Canal Street, Coatbridge, bound for Moodiesburn. This single-decker became Midland's MPE 87 and was withdrawn at the age of twelve. (A.J. Douglas)

five

Great 'Chieftain' o' the Omnibus Race

John Laurie started bus operations in 1926, concentrating on linking Hamilton with East Kilbride (then only a small village), and Eaglesham. Using a distinctive green livery with a tartan waistband, he traded under the name of Chieftain. Unlike the character played by his thespian namesake in the classic comedy *Dad's Army*, the prediction of Corporal Fraser 'We're doooooomed!!!' certainly didn't apply to the Lanarkshire Laurie and his family. His business thrived from his garage at Blantyre Road, Burnbank (west of Hamilton town centre), and when East Kilbride rapidly expanded as Scotland's first 'New Town', so too did the Chieftain routes, in addition to a network of local services within Hamilton itself. As was the common practice of many independents, Laurie bought both new and second-hand vehicles, and a variety of marques, although in the latter years of operation, Leyland was the favoured type. Chieftain was unashamedly a provider of reliable stage carriage services. Even from the early days, 'deckers dominated, and John Laurie never seemed to harbour a desire to develop any kind of coach operation.

Records show coach-bodied vehicles being rare, to say the least: A 1929 Leyland TS1, a 1934 Gilford Hera, a 1939 Albion Valkyrie, a 1960 Bedford SB, plus an eleven-seat Austin minibus bought new in 1959.

Chieftain made the headlines at the start of a new decade (1960) by buying not one but two of the then-revolutionary, rear-engined Leyland Atlanteans, becoming only the second Scottish operator to do so after Glasgow Corporation's LA 1. It wasn't until October 1961 that John Laurie's family business succumbed to takeover by Central SMT. It was the largest independent acquisition made by the nationalised outfit, and also one of their most significant. A thirty-five-strong fleet passed into Central ownership, but not Chieftain's garage. The vehicles were dispersed to Motherwell, Hamilton and East Kilbride depots. All of them saw service with Central, albeit brief for some, and others running in their old colours with CSMT fleet numbers for a time, before repainting into red and cream, or disposal.

The Laurie livery enjoyed a short revival almost three decades later, when the effects of competition post-regulation and a series of damaging strikes forced the SBG company into developing local identities. 'EK Chieftain' and 'Little Chief' were used in Hamilton and East Kilbride, adopting Chieftain's old colours.

Running empty back to the depot through Udston, Laurie's 62 was a 1948 Guy Arab II, which received a new Massey body (H30/26R) ten years later. As Central HH41, this bus ran till 1966. After withdrawal it passed via Tiger Coaches, the dealer, to AA (Dodds) Troon, who never actually used it but transferred the body on to their own CAG 800. (Photobus)

No.57 carries a full load on a Hamilton local service – Bellhaven being part of the Hillhouse district. One of a pair of 1948 Leyland PD2s bought from Yorkshire Woollen District, HD 7827 had its lifespan expanded by a further four years after the takeover as HL 187. (Photobus)

Opposite: The oldest bus which passed to Central in the sell-out was this ex-Birmingham Corporation (No.215) Leyland TD6. New in 1938, it was rebodied by English-Electric when only a few years old, and became Chieftain No.56. Pictured in Laurie's own yard, EOG 215 never carried a Central fleet number.

CHIEFTAIN
HAMILTON
Swan
72
CHIEFTAIN
KGU·433

CHIEFTAIN
PRIESTFIELD
JXN·323

Laurie's No.42 was bought new in 1956 for the East Kilbride-Eaglesham 'express' service. A Bedford SB with forty-two-seat Duple Midland body. NVD 500 became Central's C16 but was withdrawn after a year. It saw further service with Renfrewshire operator, Garners, of Bridge of Weir.

Opposite above: When Laurie sold-out to Central, virtually half the fleet was comprised of ex-London Transport buses. KGU 433 arrives in Hamilton from East Kilbride. New in 1949, this had been RTL 357 with its former owner, and as Central's HL 201 the Park-Royal bodied vehicle remained in service till 1964. In contrast to LT's detailed destination display, this was Laurie's trademark 'minimalist' lay-out, and he never used route numbers.

Opposite below: Another ex-RTL of similar vintage is seen early in its Central days, still in Chieftain colours, but now with fleet number HL/189. The bus is laying-over in Hamilton's Kemp Street. Laurie's switched their terminus to this point after local council and police chiefs had considered their previous end-point at the town's New Cross unsuitable, because of traffic volumes and the turning manoeuvres involved! Central also utilised Kemp Street in the days before the customised bus station was built in the 1970s on the other side of the railway line. Priestfield was part of High Blantyre. (A.J. Douglas)

An assortment of period cars, the street lighting, black-and-white striped road signs/bus stop all make for an evocative early-1960s scene near Hamilton's Peacock Cross. Laurie's 63 had become CSMT HL/193 and was another of the ex-LT second-hand purchases. This 1949 Leyland lasted till 1965, before being broken up by Motherwell dealer E. Corcoran. (R. Hamilton)

No.58 was a 1957 Leyland PD2 with NCME L31/28R bodywork. In its post-Chieftain days as L207, this handsome vehicle was in familiar surroundings among Central's large fleet of similar stablemates. Along with its Burnbank contemporary, MVA 100, this Chieftain bus fittingly ended its working days with the 'Highland' clan between 1969 and 1971. (A.J. Douglas)

Another Leyland, this time a highbridge PD3, is running alongside the Glasgow tramlines, after being pushed into Central service as HL/208, ironically on a route between East Kilbride and the city. This was one of the first of the type to be built by Leyland in 1957, and it carried a seventy-three-seat body. The billboards carry an appropriate assortment of contemporary advertisements. (R. Hamilton)

Although Leyland built the chassis on this PD3/2 in 1957, they retained it for development work for two years before selling it to Laurie, who specified the Massey forward-entrance bodywork. It is caught here in East Kilbride passing Central's L314, before Chieftain 69 joined the 'red bus' fleet as HL/209. After withdrawal in 1967, UVA 638 enjoyed a 'gypsy' existence with several operators around the country: Derwent Coaches, Swalwell; then back North to Rennie's, Dunfermline; and eventually to Laverty of Neilston. Whilst in Fife, Rennie performed major surgery on this bus, firstly replacing its damaged roof with that from an ex-Alexander (Fife) Bristol LD, and then replacing the Pneumocyclic gearbox in 1973 with a syncromesh 'box. (A.J. Douglas)

As Chieftain No.41, WVD 340 was the first new coach bought by Laurie in over two decades. A Bedford SB1 from 1960, this vehicle suffered major damage two years after takeover, and had to have a replacement Duple forty-one-seat body fitted by Central. Their C15, it was withdrawn in 1966, and was bought by Baird's of Dunoon in the following year.

This was the second half of the Chieftain pair to set tongues wagging among transport chiefs and the travelling public alike in Lanarkshire. Glasgow Corporation deployed its first Leyland Atlantean in 1958, and although the municipal operator followed up with huge orders from 1962, it was John Laurie who showed the spirit of enterprise when he took delivery of No.77 (XVA 444) in 1960 and No.78 just months before takeover by Central. Both buses had MCCW H44/33F bodywork, and, when transferred into the CSMT fleet as HR1/2, became the SBG's first Atlanteans. No.78 (60 AVA) climbs out of Hamilton en route to Hairmyres Hospital via E. Kilbride. This vehicle passed to A1 Services member Steele of Stevenson in 1969, and was sadly scrapped less than five years later. Sister bus XVA 444 was sold on to Graham's of Paisley, also in 1969. (R. Hamilton)

six

Wilson's – 'The Wonder Years'!

The Wilson family's association with buses dates back as far as the 1920s when they ran, albeit for a fairly short time, in the Peebles and Galashiels area. Operations then transferred to Whitelees, Lanark, under the name of the Gala Motor Transport Company, with a route network serving the surrounding areas. In 1932, Gala was acquired by Central SMT, but within a few years, Robert Wilson re-started the business, this time based in the 'deep south' of Lanarkshire at Carnwath, where they would remain for a further sixty-plus years. Local services, Private Hire and other work grew steadily, including a cross-country route from Forth to Edinburgh, terminating in the capital at Castle Terrace, which Wilson had commenced in 1946. Town Services in Carluke were also operated. In the summer of 1966, the company successfully took over the grant-aided service of Jack McKnight, linking the eighteenth-century Industrial Revolution village of New Lanark with the county town itself (Lanark).

Increasing car ownership and decreasing passenger numbers saw the clouds of uncertainty loom ominously over Wilson's (and other small operators across the country), but a new decade brought a change of fortunes to the Carnwath company. 1970 saw two significant takeovers – Dempster of Larkhall, and John Dodds of Lesmahagow. With these acquisitions not only came vehicles, but more importantly licences for works services and tours. Dempster also owned a prime garage site at Canderside Toll, near the A/M74. The business of Wilson McClure of far-distant Glenmavis was bought over in 1973, yielding a 'Workers' Express' service from Airdrie/Coatbridge to the College Milton Industrial Estate in East Kilbride, primarily serving the employees of the BSR factory.

The takeovers concluded with Wilson's acquiring the six vehicles and works/tours licences of Palmer of Douglas in 1975. The company bought many vehicle marques over the decades, and tended to keep some buses for years. From the 1970s, the policy appeared to focus on not purchasing coaches new, but second-hand single-/double-deck buses. The livery has been a distinctive maroon/red and white/cream and the addition of grey on 'deckers was not maintained. The final livery, out with the time span of this book, was red/yellow.

Despite surviving through further difficult times during the next two decades, Wilson's reached their own terminus in 2001, and are much-missed in bus/coach operations in South Lanarkshire.

Two views taken at the same spot in Carluke, but a few years apart, and both showing former Hutchison's of Overtown vehicles which Wilson had bought and were using on the Town Services. Note the changes at the location in the lower view: the corrugated roof building has been demolished, and the 'corner shop' is now displaying a contemporary sign for Walls' Ice Cream. The Austin A-35 saloon is 'replaced' by a Mini Van.
Above: A Duple-bodied Albion Victor.
Below: A Bedford C5, also with bodywork by Duple. (Both A.J. Douglas)

Opposite: A second-hand Ford Thames with the uncommon Bellhouse-Hartwell thirty-seat coach body was regularly used on the 'trunk' service across to Edinburgh. The route was abandoned in 1967, the year after this vehicle had been sold and converted into a mobile shop by its new owner in Hamilton. (A.J. Douglas)

Although it had been new to Paterson of Dalry, this Commer Beadle integral single-decker also came to Wilson's via Hutchison. It was for use on the former Jack McKnight service. The route out of the picturesque New Lanark is tortuous – a narrow road, sharp bends and a very steep incline. Industrialists Robert Owen and David Dale built the village around the latter's eighteenth-century cotton mill. It was in decline by the time Wilson took over the subsidised route, with population dwindling as low as only 100 in 1972. Thankfully, a long-term restoration project has resulted in the village being 'saved' and it is now thriving again as a popular tourist attraction with Conservation Trust status. The same can't be said for the little bus. (A.J. Douglas)

One of the most interesting 'deckers in the Wilson fleet was this AEC. Hanson's converted it from a Regal III to a Regent III with a then-new Roe body in 1953. It ran for Huddersfield Corporation who acquired the Yorkshire operator, before passing to Wilson's. It is seen here, late in its Lanarkshire life, in the Depot yard at Carnwath. (K.T. Langhorn)

By a strange twist of fate, after stopping their service to Edinburgh in 1967, Wilson operated several ex-Lothian Region Transport vehicles some years later. The first, LFS 439, came in the Palmer's takeover in 1975. Seen here on the Lanark road, this Leyland PD 2 carries the full grey/maroon/white 'decker livery used for a time, and has Metro Cammell Orion bodywork. (A.J. Douglas)

During 1976/77, Wilson's acquired four Leyland PD3's from LRT. All had been new in 1964 with Alexander bodies, and ex-Lothian 684 is well-laden on a Private Hire with its new owners, carrying the re-vamped 'Wilson's Supreme Travel' legend. (A.J. Douglas)

Another unusual acquisition was LVA 552, an Albion Victor with Strachan thirty-two-seat body, which came from Whiteford of Lanark in 1969. It is laying-over at Lanark Railway Station, which is quite apt. Doesn't the front of this bus look like a 'face' of a 'Thomas the Tank Engine' character? (A.J. Douglas)

Above: Another Albion, this time a short Harrington-bodied Nimbus, was purchased in December 1972 from English operator Hutchings & Cornelius, for use on the Lanark/New Lanark service. Climbing Wellgatehead in the town, the thirty-one-seat bus is followed by the last model of stylish Ford Zephyr. (A.J. Douglas)

Opposite middle: As well as second-hand Leyland 'deckers, Wilson's also brought Dennis Lolines to Carnwath from English operators in the summer of 1974. This Alexander-bodied bus had been in the Alder Valley fleet. The Corporation housing in the background suggests 454 EDT has been snapped on a football fans' hire in Glasgow. (A.J. Douglas)

Opposite below: Bristol double-deckers had been a common sight in Lanarkshire for years, thanks to Central SMT, but Wilson was the county's first independent to acquire an FLF. An autumn day inside one of Glasgow's many parks is the setting for SRB 64F, which had come from Mansfield & District. (A.J. Douglas)

Right: Vehicle variety was always evident in the Wilson's fleet, which by late 1979 was thirty-four-strong. 44 KUA was one of a trio of ex-Grampian AEC Reliances bought in 1976. All three had bodywork by Roe, with forty-one seats and double doors. As the blind hints, this bus had been running on a Carluke local.

Parked-up in the depot yard, this pristine pair of Leyland PD3A's came from West Yorkshire PTE in 1978, where they'd been Nos 2243/2244. The stylish H40/30F bodywork is by Neepsend.

Three former Greater Glasgow PTE Atlanteans headed for a more rural home in 1979. MUS 274F had been new in 1967 to Glasgow Corporation, and carried the 'standard' Alexander seventy-eight-seat bodywork. (K.T. Langhorn)

seven

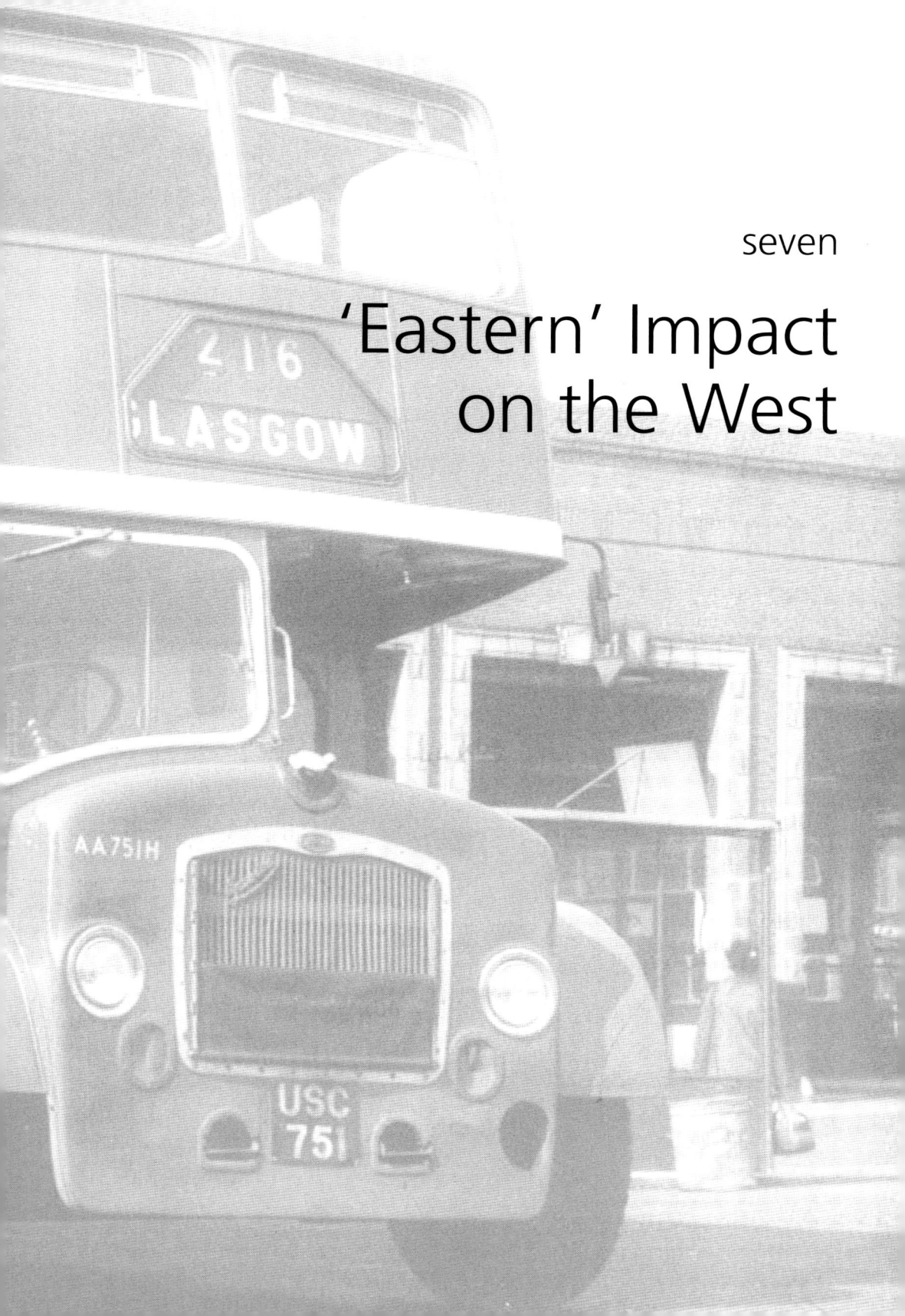

'Eastern' Impact on the West

While Central was the major nationalised operator in the county, another member of the SBG played a significant role in North Lanarkshire – Scottish Omnibuses Ltd. (SOL), later of course renamed Eastern Scottish. This company was already referred to in Chapter two, with their take-over of Baxter's Bus Services, but SOL's presence in the Airdrie/Coatbridge area dates back to the 1930s.

'Pioneer' busman John Sword had established a depot for his Midland Bus Services at Clarkston to cover the network of routes to Glasgow, Slamannan, Longriggend, Newmains. In 1932, Midland was one of the major foundation companies for Western SMT, and Mr Sword became Western's manager. Three years later, the Airdrie operation, services and vehicles were transferred to the SMT Co. (The Western presence did live on for some decades in the sole shape of the long trunk service No.42 from Airdrie to Ayr via Kilmarnock, and they maintained an outstation in the former Currie & Thomson depot at Calderbank, by Airdrie, till the late fifties.)

The garage in Connor Street, Clarkston served as a good base for SMT/SOL to operate several services to Glasgow from Caldercruix, Longriggend, Clarkston and Chapelhall, in addition to the inter-city service from Glasgow to Edinburgh via Bathgate (No.16). The operation of the last route was shared with Bathgate depot. The company also maintained other more local services inherited from Western, and over a period of years expanded them. As Airdrie's housing schemes grew, so too did SOL's service provision on 'town' services, covering routes not provided by Baxter's.

The only real competition with the well-established local company was between Airdrie and Coatbridge, simply because all of SOL's Glasgow Services, plus their routes to Muirhead (245) and Gartcosh (246) ran on the main A89 road which links the towns. Most of the Airdrie 'Town Routes' terminated at Gartlea Bus Station, but a couple extended to Gartleahill, a large council estate. Other services ran to Glenmavis, Greengairs, Whitburn, O'wood (Holytown) and Newmains. Some had been inherited with the acquisition of the W. Irvine of Glenmavis business in 1940. When SOL, which became Eastern Scottish in 1964, ceased their Baxter operation in 1977, Victoria Garage continued to be used for a time, and green-liveried vehicles did carry the 'V' depot suffix, until all were transferred up the road to Clarkston.

The reorganisation of the Scottish Bus Group in 1985, saw Connor Street becoming a Central Scottish depot, and then Kelvin Central Buses four years later. Clarkston garage finally closed in 1996 and has since been demolished. The site is now occupied by private housing, with no reminder left of its former existence. After the takeover of Lowland Motorways of Shettleston in 1958, and with subsequent additional services in and around the east side of Glasgow, SOL built a new depot at Baillieston that opened in 1960. This too is long gone. Since Baillieston was on the Glasgow City boundary and the routes run from there primarily served Glasgow itself, this chapter concentrates on the SOL/Eastern Scottish operations centred on Clarkston.

Opposite: SOL inherited several ex-London Transport RT's with the Lowland takeover. JXC 220 was a Cravens-bodied AEC Regent III from 1949, and was also re-allocated to Connor Street. As BB3H, it is set to leave Airdrie stance for Newmains, a service which was later extended to Law Hospital. This bus returned south to meet is fate in a breaker's yard at Wombwell, South Yorkshire, in 1964. (R. Marshall)

Above: Before Baillieston Garage was built, some of the ex-Lowland Motorways acquisitions found their way to Clarkston, depot code 'H'. Pictured on the peripheries of Gartlea Bus Station is GAT 62 (HH3), one of a pair of former East Yorkshire Leyland TD5s, new in 1939 and given ECW bodies in 1948. On a local service to Whinhall, this bus wears the light green/cream livery, and still carries the famous SMT diamond logo. It was withdrawn in 1962.

Parked-up at the back of Gartlea stance next to Broomfield Park, home of the original Airdrieonians' FC, is HH6 H. This all-Leyland PD2 was only four years old when SOL bought-out Lowland. It lasted with its new owners till 1970, having been transferred back to the new Baillieston garage (C) to run over its old stamping ground. The Milk Marketing Board advert on the side-panel adorned scores of SBG vehicles in the early 1960s.

The 'Eastern Scottish' name and dark (Lothian) green/cream livery was introduced in 1964, as shown here on NSG 818. Ready to leave for Greengairs, a former mining village three miles north of Airdrie, this single-decker was a 1956 AEC Monocoach with Alexander forty-one-seat body. As B527 it lasted till 1972.

As with Central, SOL also jumped on the 'Bristol bandwagon'. OWS 604 was an LD6G model of 1957 vintage. As AA604H, it wears a variant of the 'new' ES livery, with no cream band on the front panel under the destination screen. Shown here leaving Gartlea for Whitburn, this bus gave eighteen years service. (A.J. Douglas)

With more than a touch of irony, this 1959 Bristol spent the last five years of its SOL life in Baxter's colours, working out of Victoria Garage from 1971. In this view as a Connor Street vehicle, AA726 appears to have been on a short-working of the 217 from Glasgow, but ending at Airdrie Cross instead of Clarkston, no doubt to be re-deployed from the stance on an Airdrie local service. This bus was bought by the Craigmillar Festival Society in Edinburgh in 1976, before being broken up by an English dealer two years later. (Photobus)

In the bus park at Glasgow's Killermont Street, AA751 has worked the 216 from Caldercruix, a village east of Airdrie which was once home to a large paper mill. Note the Travel Press & Publicity (SBG's own company) advert extolling the virtues of touring Britain by Coach. USC 751 was a 1960 LD with H33/27RD ECW body, and had a fifteen-year working life. (S. Kelly)

The penultimate LD6G model for SOL, bought new in 1961, is pictured in its latter days in the depot yard at Clarkston. Although working the 215 from Glasgow to Longriggend, AA858H has pulled into Connor Street either for a crew change or a 'comfort' stop! Another former mining village beyond Airdrie, Longriggend was home for many years to a Remand Unit/Young Offenders Institution, which has since been closed. (Photobus)

Working the cross-country Glasgow-Edinburgh via Bathgate route, DD695 is on the South Circular Road in Coatbridge, formerly Canal Street (pre-town centre redevelopment). Although fitted with 'PAYE' signs, this service was still crew-operated in the late 1970s. KSX 695N was an ECW-bodied Daimler Fleetline, delivered new in 1975. (K.T. Langhorn)

A somewhat misleading picture! Despite the Ayrshire registration, the 'Prestwick' half-showing in the screen and the 'A' suffix indicating Edinburgh New Street, this bus is actually caught on camera in Coatbridge. It was one of sixteen 'Y' type bodied Leyland Leopards transferred from Western SMT in 1969. Originally C36FT, ZH 385 was reseated to forty-nine. It had been 1831 in its previous owner's fleet.

N864 was part of the first batch of Leyland Nationals bought by SOL in 1978. It is seen here at the side of the new Gartlea Bus Station (not in view) on the former Baxter's service to Kirkshaws in Coatbridge, and is one-man operated. The construction of new justiciary buildings in the early 1970s saw the old Gartlea Bus Station demolished, and moved across the road to another purpose built layout. The 'new' station has now also disappeared to make way for a retail unit, leaving Airdrie without a bus stance. (Policy Transport Photographs)

Laying-over in a bay within the newer Bus Stance, JSF 906T has just arrived on the 245 service from Muirhead. ZS906 was a Seddon VII new in 1978, with Alexander 'T' type forty-nine-seat body. (D.G. MacDonald)

eight

Stokes – Smooth Operators!

The Stokes name has been synonymous with transport in South Lanarkshire since the 1920s. It was in this decade that the company founder William started off from his shop using a hand cart to deliver fruit and vegetables which had been brought from the Fruit Markets in both Glasgow and Edinburgh, before progressing to motorised lorries and general haulage. Eventually, the family moved into bus operation using two Bedford OB's to transport miners to the local pits. Two stage-carriage services remained the backbone of the Stokes business for many years: Lanark to Lesmahagow, and Lanark to Coalburn. It's interesting that the terminal 'home' point of both these routes was Lanark, some five miles away from Stokes' base at Carstairs Village. Second-hand double-deckers from a variety of sources ran on these services, still supplemented by workers' runs and a sprinkling of private hires.

As with some other companies featured in this book, this was always secondary to bus operations, highlighted by the practice of hiring/borrowing a vehicle from village neighbour Henderson's, in the days when Stokes had no genuine coaches.

Home to the State Mental Hospital, Carstairs has always been more famous as a major railway junction. Despite the rural location, it was fairly well served by both Central SMT, and SOL/Eastern Scottish, the latter because the village was on their cross-country route from Lanark to Edinburgh.

At one point William Stokes and his son Alex, considered setting-up across in the capital, and actually used a travel agent's office as a base to take bookings for hires. The main obstacle to this idea being a long-term success was the refusal of Edinburgh Council chiefs to allow Stokes to have garage/depot premises within Auld Reekie. They were 'outsiders' from Lanarkshire, albeit a neighbouring county to the Lothian area, but not Edinburgh fowk!

Whilst the haulage business didn't appear to present too many problems, the bus operations did. The remote location and routes meant for difficult winter conditions every year. Allied to that, a decreasing population in the locale and the declining coal industry forced Stokes to advertise the PSV business for sale in 1969. However, a U-turn was made when Whiteford of Lanark abandoned his Lanark-Lesmahagow via Kirkfieldbank route, a service which Whiteford had acquired in 1962 from Jackson, of Auchenheath.

Although this run crossed the Clyde Valley it was less difficult and busier than Stokes' own route, and that's what made the Carstairs operator have a change of heart. Stokes took over this service in 1970 and made slight changes within the Lesmahagow end of the journey. OMO was introduced full-scale the following year, and thereafter the company continued to prosper once again. Stokes' mainly red livery, similar to BET, was revamped in 1975 to a half-red, half-cream scheme, which is still used today. Notable exceptions to the previous all-red rule were two former Southdown Leyland Royal Tiger Coaches which retained green livery and the legend, 'Stokes Travelways'.

The company remains a solid operator to this day, still based in Carstairs, but with a larger network of stage services, plus school contracts and Private Hire work. It is also pleasing to note that the Stokes family still own the business, with the late founder's grandsons Robert & Walter, and the latter's wife Wilma, looking after the entire operation.

Opposite above: Buses bought by Stokes tended to enjoy long lives, and this Leyland TD7 was already twenty-three years old when acquired from Southdown in 1961. With Park Royal bodywork, EUF 162 is crossing the River Clyde via Kirkfieldbank Bridge, heading for Coalburn. (A.J. Douglas)

Left middle: An interesting characteristic of the company's purchasing policy was the buying of buses in pairs. These two pictures show a pair of AEC Regents, which had been with Rhondda Valley, but acquired by Stokes via a Yorkshire dealer. (R. Marshall)

Left below: This view captures Lanark Bus Station in its heyday, the 1960s. HTG 709 is flanked by an AEC Monocoach of SOL, and a Central Bristol LD6G. The two clippies in shot are Central staff, as Stokes crew didn't wear bespoke uniforms. Two sisters who worked as conductresses for the independent did create their own trend by wearing cardigans back-to-front. (Photobus)

Making for Lanark through the Clyde Valley countryside is LKG 213. This was a Leyland Olympian new in 1956 to Western Welsh. It has a Weymann B44F body, and carries the shortened 'Stokes' lettering, which succeeded the earlier fleet-name of 'Stokes Bus Services' (A.J. Douglas)

On a cold, grey day, ECK 870 climbs out of Kirkfieldbank, the village at the eastern end of the Clyde Valley on the south bank. This 1951 Leyland PD2 had been new to Scout's of Preston, and the bus stayed with Stokes till 1968. The intermediate destinations of 'Rigside' and 'Douglas Water' on the display show its coming back to Lanark from Coalburn, a journey which took fifty-two minutes, but occasionally longer in bad weather. (A.J. Douglas)

Parked-up at the back of Lanark stance is a 1950 Leyland PD2/3 with L27/26RD bodywork, which Stokes bought from Ribble Motor Services where it had been fleet No.2733. The Seddon truck belonged to Smith's Bellshill Haulage Limited, who, like Central SMT no longer exists. (A.J. Douglas)

Under the watchful eye of a sergeant from the old Lanarkshire Constabulary, HWS 777 climbs Lanark High Street at the end of its run from Lesmahagow. This single-decker was one of a pair of 1952 Leyland Royal Tigers which came from Edinburgh Corporation in the summer of 1967. It had been No.113 with its previous owner. (A.J. Douglas)

A pair of posers in the depot yard at Carstairs as further proof of Stokes' belief in buying buses in two's. VCH 173/175 were Leyland Tiger Cubs which came north in 1972 from Trent Motor Services. Both had Willowbrook dual-purpose forty-one-seat bodywork. The coach on the left is one half of the duo of former Southdown Duple-bodied Leylands which continued to wear their previous owners colours. (A.J. Douglas)

An early 1970s shot in Lanark shows 242 GTJ carrying Stokes' 'old' livery. This vehicle has Burlingham C41F coachwork, and was one of a pair – inevitably – which was bought from Lancashire United late in 1970. (A.J. Douglas)

Destined for 'The Gow', as Lesmahagow is known to the locals, OCD 774 climbs out of the Clyde Valley. This Leyland Titan was the last 'decker taken out of service when Stokes converted to OMO. New to Southdown, it had a Park Royal fifty-seven-seat body, and was fitted with rear platform doors. (A.J. Douglas)

Another ex-Southdown acquisition, also with Park Royal bodywork, PUF 634 was a Guy Arab. The bus is pictured carrying a full load on a Day Trip, possibly a school outing judging by the youthful faces. (A.J. Douglas)

Arguably the most interesting pair bought by Stokes were two AEC Swifts new in 1968 to Sheffield, with Park Royal forty-nine-seat, two door bodies. Although entered into service in their original condition, Stokes wanted them converted to a single-door layout. Local firm Stewarts were given the first bus, but because the Wishaw coachbuilder took so long to complete the job, Stokes did the second conversion themselves. Just after repainting, TWE 21F is in the yard at Carstairs. At the time, they were the only rear-engined buses operated by a Lanarkshire independent. (Photobus)

Photographed when almost new, Plaxton bodied Leyland Leopard coach HGE 51T is representative of the vehicles bought by Stokes in the late 1970s. (Photobus)

nine

The Irvine Influence

Like Hutchisons, Stokes and Baxter's, another family whose renown and reputation as bus and coach operators has been respected for decades, is the Irvine dynasty. Sharing a name only with an Ayrshire town, the Irvine family history is well and truly rooted in the coalfields of Lanarkshire, and the village of Salsburgh, between Airdrie and Shotts.

The Miners' Strike of the Depression Era in the 1920s forced Peter Irvine, himself all too familiar with the pit-face, into rethinking how he could provide for his large family of twelve. He decided on transport and in 1926 went into business using a solitary seventeen-seat Reo (an American bus, once quite popular in the UK). A service to Airdrie from his home village was soon set-up, and that was followed by Private Hire work, which expanded the operation and fleet considerably over the years. Perhaps ironically, Irvine also ferried miners to the local pits, till the industry eventually died in the area. By the 1950s, the 'Golden Eagle' name was well established, and the red/maroon and cream vehicles easily recognised in the locale and further beyond. The fleet had always been dominated by new vehicles, and that policy was to continue when son John took over the reins from his father Peter. The company did have some second-hand purchases, and they actually had other members of the family running a dealer's business.

Pictured on a Day Trip to Girvan when new in 1951, GVA 115 was a Leyland Royal Tiger with Duple C41C bodywork. The driver is wearing his 'summer' lightweight jacket in grey. Irvine used the traditional-type black uniform, similar to that worn by SBG employees. (Irvine family)

Opposite above: This 'Tiger' roared a bit further than Girvan – here it is being hoisted on board for a tour to Switzerland, long before the ro-ro ferries. Note the magnificent eagle motif, which adorned all the coaches at that time. (Irvine family)

Buses obviously ran in the blood of all Peter Irvine's sons, because three others, Robert, William and Thomas set up Tiger Coaches in 1947, and although they ultimately became a dealer/breaker, they did have a few coaches licensed directly to Irvine Bros (Tiger Coaches) for Private Hire work only, mainly a miners' contract. By 1955 Robert was the sole proprietor of Tiger Coaches and decided to concentrate on trading vehicles.

Left: One of the vehicles on the 'Tiger' Licence was this 1948 Foden PVSC6. Bought new, this vehicle was given a thirty-five-seat coach body actually built by the Irvine family at Salsburgh, a feat repeated on several occasions around that time with vehicles for the main fleet. As with 'Golden Eagle, the motif depicting the 'Tiger' was impressive. (Irvine family)

Initially based at Dewshill, just on the outskirts of Salsburgh, Robert Irvine moved the Tiger Coaches operation to a yard at the eastern end of the village Main Street. As a dealer/breaker, Tiger handled disposals from many companies, including Central, Glasgow and Edinburgh Corporation. Central's HL188, a former Chieftain 'decker awaits its fate. Son Graham now runs the Tiger operation from the same yard.

Returning to the Golden Eagle fleet, and another coach bodied by Irvine at Salsburgh. EVD 907 was a Guy Vixen new in 1949, and it carried fleet No.31. (Irvine family)

Above: From the less-picturesque Salsburgh to a far-flung corner of France, KVD 827 is well-travelled in this late fifties snap. The coach was one of three Bedford SBO's bought new in 1955 with Duple thirty-six-seat bodies. (Irvine family)

In 1959, Irvine's acquired the business of J. Greenshields, another native of Salsburgh, who had begun operating around the same time as Peter Irvine. With the take-over came the Shotts-Airdrie service, longer obviously than Irvine's own run from Salsburgh and four vehicles, one of which is pictured below.

Below: Laying-over at Airdrie before heading out to Shotts, the most handsome vehicle from the take-over was surely this AEC Regent V. New in 1959, SVD 676 carried the stylish Massey L31/28R bodywork. (A.J. Douglas)

Although never the dominant force, double-deckers did play an important part in Irvine's operation, particularly at peak times when the pits were still at their prime. Pictured in front of the garage is MVD 627, a 1956 Leyland PD2/12 with Northern Counties lowbridge body. No doubt when this bus travelled to Airdrie it was oft-times mistaken for a vehicle from the Western or Central fleets! It met a premature end after an accident, which made it a write-off. (R.F. Mack)

Irvine's indulged in occasional second-hand purchases, as shown here by CCK 375. This Leyland PD2 had been new in 1948 to Ribble, Preston. Note the floodlight pylon and stand roof in the background of Broomfield Park, the old home of Airdrieonians F.C. (R.H.G. Simpson)

In the early 1960s, before the coal industry burned out, Irvine bought two 11m (36ft) AEC Reliances for use on both services into Airdrie. 652 GVA had fifty-five seats on a Plaxton body. It saw further service with Colchester Corporation.

Willing to be innovative, Peter Irvine invested in a pair of lightweight Bedford VAL14's in 1965, with fifty-four-seat bodies by Willowbrook. Long-serving Fleet engineer (and ex-driver) David Thomson, who's spent his entire working life with Irvine's, recalls the twin-steer buses lacked stamina, and cost a fortune in frequently replaced brake parts! Needless to say, their Salsburgh stay was brief. (R.H.G. Simpson)

Heading through Salsburgh, at the Eastern end of Main Street, WVA 453 was half of a pair of AEC Reliances with Willowbrook B45F bodies. New in 1960, both buses passed to OK Motor Services, Bishop Auckland just five years later.

For the era covered by this book, AEC was Irvine's favoured marque, both for buses and coaches. YVA 870 sits inside the depot gates. This coach and its sister YVA 871 were diverted from Hutchison of Overtown's order in 1961. The pair were Reliance coaches with the distinctive Duple Britannia forty-one-seat bodies. (A.J. Douglas)

Late in 1966/early in 1967, Irvine's bought a total of eight ex-London Transport 'deckers, some of which were pressed into service still in LT red. Four were RTL's and the other four were AEC Regent III's, as shown here in KGK 757/776. The last double-decker was withdrawn in 1972. (A.J. Douglas)

The by-then rapid decline of the mining industry forced the company into a slight policy change. The two long-bodied Reliances and the uneconomic Bedford VAL's (p.107) were replaced in 1966 by a quartet of AH470-engined Reliances with forty-five bus seats by Marshall. These vehicles gave over a decade of sterling service. Second of the batch, HVA 866D pulls into Airdrie Bus Stance from Salsburgh. (R.H.G. Simpson)

Above: Despite their frequent use, Irvine's buses in general and the AEC's in particular were so reliable. This was due in no small part to the company's high standards of maintenance and cleaning. It was 1970 before the next new buses were delivered, a pair of forty-seven-seat Reliances with bodies by Plaxton. Seen when new, VVD 64H carries a PAYE. sign, but Irvine's didn't introduce OMO till 1972. The expansion of Newhouse Industrial Estate and the Shotts service operating via Chapelhall helped lift passenger levels.

Although they ceased stage-carriage work in 1994, Golden Eagle is still very much to the local fore, with a fifteen-strong fleet of coaches deployed on Private Hire, Contract and Schools work. The Garage on Salsburgh's Main Street has been partly-rebuilt and the business is still owned by the Irvine family – Peter, Robert and Ishbel – grandchildren of the founder Peter.

When the trio of Irvine brothers who'd set up Tiger Coaches went their own ways in the mid-1950s, William moved into the car trade in Glasgow but he returned to the bus industry in May 1958 when he bought over the old-established business of Adam Duncan in Law, a village between Wishaw and Carluke, and services linking those two towns. Using initially a maroon and off-white colour scheme, 'Post Office' Red was also introduced to the livery. Private Hire work was developed during the sixties using a pair of Ford coaches. After William's death in 1968, his widow Mary and son Peter took over the licences, and expansion of the fleet was necessitated by the securing of more schools and contract work. The company has always bought a mix of new and second-hand vehicles, and from the mid-1970s the intake has been more of a dual-purpose role because of the variety of work.

Above: With the Duncan business came two Guy Arab IV 'deckers, one with Massey body, the other shown here with Strachan's bodywork. HVA 876 is about to pick-up a heavy passenger load on Wishaw's Stewarton Street, Irvine's 'stance', although the blind has still to be turned for the return journey to Carluke via Law. (A.J. Douglas)

Opposite below: A landmark picture in many ways, AUS 418S enters the 'new' Airdrie Bus Station in 1979. This was the very last AEC Reliance bought by John Irvine in 1978 before he standardised on Volvos and Leyland. It carried a Marshall B51F body. The vehicle wears the brighter version of the red livery introduced at the start of the decade, and the fleet name 'Golden Eagle Coaches'. This scene has changed almost beyond recognition – the 'new' Gartlea Stance has been demolished and replaced by a retail outlet, while Safeway's supermarket occupies the site of the football stadium. The only reminder of its former occupant is the in-store Post Office named 'Broomfield' (A.J. Douglas)

Two second-hand purchases from Ribble Motor Services, both AEC Reliances with Marshall bodies.

Above: UCK 498 is in Station Road in Law outside the original A. Duncan depot. Irvine moved in 1990 to their current Lawmuir Road purpose-built garage in the middle of Law Village. (K. Langhorn)

Below: Passing Wishaw Police Station on a wet day ARN 570C also carries 48 the number allocated to the company's main run of Carluke-Wishaw via Law. This was actually two services operating effectively as one: Wishaw – Law via Law Hospital (now closed) ran half-hourly for much of the day, while the more rural Law-Carluke stretch had a bus every ninety minutes. (A.J. Douglas)

Peter Irvine has always had an eye for a bargain, and is an enthusiast, as well as being a good businessman. (He also has a passion for restoring Classic Cars.) He's always enjoyed renovating second-hand bus purchases before selling-on. JLA 61D was a prime example of this. An AEC Merlin with double-doors new to London Transport (XMS Class) as a standee saloon, Irvine converted it to B51F before disposal, as shown here.

Seen on a Day Trip, NVD 725L typifies the intake during the 1970s. New to Parks of Hamilton, where it had also been a team coach for Rangers FC, this vehicle was a Volvo B58 with 11m. Duple Dominant body. The elderly Morris Minor car in-shot is also noteworthy. (R.H.G. Simpson)

Above: Like Hutchison, tight timetables meant Irvine still deployed crew operation till some time after 1979. Heading down Wishaw Main Street, MUS 104P was a Duple-bodied Leyland Leopard bought from Garelochhead Coach Services, Dunbartonshire where it had been their fleet No.131.

Left: Throughout its relatively short history, the Irvine fleet has always had varied and unusual vehicles. One of the most interesting, surely, would have to be this Leyland Titan PD3. FKY 243E came to Law via Wilson of Carnwath. It had been new to West Yorkshire PTE (2243) and carried a Neepsend H40/30F body. (K. Langhorn)

Since the passing of his mother in 1980, Peter Irvine has been in sole control of what is still a thriving bus and coach business. Private Hire and Schools Contracts are still an integral part of the operation, and in the days since deregulation, more services have been added, both within Lanarkshire and into Glasgow. In a fitting twist, Irvine of Law now operates the Airdrie-Salsburgh/Shotts route abandoned by his North Lanarkshire cousins in 1994.

ten

Clyde Valley Variety

In addition to the operators covered so far, a further assortment of mainly smaller firms held a creditable place in Lanarkshire's public transport network. Some ran stage-carriage services, while others provided workers', miners' and other contract services, as well as private hire work.

Hamilton ('Hammy') Jackson, a native of the remote village of Auchenheath, operated a service from Lanark to Lesmahagow.

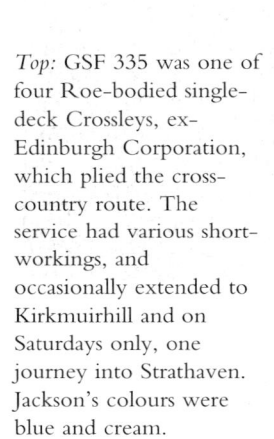

Top: GSF 335 was one of four Roe-bodied single-deck Crossleys, ex-Edinburgh Corporation, which plied the cross-country route. The service had various short-workings, and occasionally extended to Kirkmuirhill and on Saturdays only, one journey into Strathaven. Jackson's colours were blue and cream. (A.J. Douglas)

Middle: In 1962, Jackson sold the stage service and three of the Crossley single-deckers to Whiteford of Lanark, but he retained his coaching operation for almost another decade. This pair of Crossley coaches with Santus bodywork survived until 1965. (A.J. Douglas)

Bottom: Passing through Larkhall on a Private Hire, TWJ 251 was an AEC Reliance acquired in 1965, with a then-stylish Duple C41C body. (A.J. Douglas)

Another single-service provider was Jack McKnight, linking Robert Owen's Industrial Revolution 'model' village of New Lanark with 'The Marches' area of Lanark itself. Despite the steep hill and a dangerously-sharp hairpin bend, McKnight did use an ex-Glasgow Corporation 'decker, which replaced an ex-Western Leyland Titan, but single-decks were the norm. Jack McKnight, whose premises were in New Lanark, sold out to Wilson's of Carnwath in 1966.

Above: Picking-up passengers in Lanark, ERN 806 was one of two Duple-bodied Commer Commandos regularly used on McKnight's service (R. Marshall)

Below: On the opposite side of Lanark's High Sreet, HWO 357 (and its sister 358) was an Albion Valiant which McKnight purchased second-hand in 1965 from Welsh operator Edwards of Lhybrook, but had been new to Red & White. (A.J. Douglas)

James Whiteford & Sons had been in existence since the 1930s as an excursions and tours operator, adjunct to a haulage business in Nemphlar on the fringes of Lanark. When the 'Sons', Robert and Ian, took the reins after their father's passing, they further developed the business with stage carriage, miners' and schools services as well as Private Hire.

Whiteford's took over Hammy Jackson's service in 1962. On a rural road KVA 39 heads for Strathaven, on the Saturday-only run. This was an Alexander-bodied Leyland Tiger Cub which had been new to Hutchison's. (A.J. Douglas)

At the same time as acquiring Jackson's service, Whiteford took over the business of Mrs M. Love of Lesmahagow, trading as Hugh Love. As well as important miners' contracts, came several vehicles, including this Manchester-style all-Crossley 'decker. Seen in Lanark, in early 1963 DVA 670, which had been new to Adam Duncan of Law, still wears Love's livery, and just to confuse even more, has paper stickers proclaiming 'Jacksons Bus Service', indicating it was on Hammy's old run, now operated by Whiteford. (A.J. Douglas)

While buses were second-hand buys, the majority of Whiteford's coaching stock was purchased new. Carrying branding for Continental Hire, FVA 679D was the first of three Ford R192's with Plaxton Panorma forty-five-seat bodies in 1966. (A.J. Douglas)

Still carrying Ribble colours and front-end nameplate, ECK 576 heads down Lanark High Street. A forty-four-seat Leyland Royal Tiger, it had been No.313 in the Ribble fleet. Note the '007' display – shurely shome mishtake, Miss Moneypenny!! (A.J. Douglas)

In the early 1970s, Whiteford's sold the stage service to Stokes, but continued Private Hire work, becoming a Scottish subsidiary of World Wide Coaches, touring both at home and abroad. Whiteford's left WWC in 1977 and became Nationwide Coaches, but sold out in 1988 to Wilson's, Carnwath, who'd already taken over their works contracts in the previous decade.

Robert Duncan of Motherwell was a man of many interests. He owned two grocers' shops, a small haulage business, and operated buses and coaches. From his premises almost literally in the shadow of Central SMT's Traction House HQ, Duncan ran a mixture of 'deckers and coaches. Private Hire, Miners' and Factory Contracts provided the main trade, but the company was regularly sub-contracted, not by neighbours Central, but by Western SMT to take holidaymakers to Blackpool, from both Glasgow and Edinburgh.

Most of Duncan's 'deckers were second-hand acquisitions, such as this ex-London Transport RTL 575, bought in 1967. (A.J. Douglas)

Similar to the batch purchased by Central, GM 6322 was a 1954 Leyland PD2 actually ordered and bought new by Duncan. (A.J. Douglas)

Latterly run by the late founder's son-in-law, the company no longer operates, but the garage and yard at the start of 'The Loaning' in Motherwell are still in family ownership and stand empty as a reminder of another respected, local business.

A driver with Central SMT at Traction House, John Dodds was a cousin of the Ayrshire independent, Dodds of Troon, and he became an omnibus owner in his own right when he took over the business of Larkhall's Jimmy Yuill, who wanted to concentrate on haulage. Deployed principally on workers' contracts, including Rolls-Royce in East Kilbride and Daks-Simpson in Larkhall, and Miners' services, Dodds utilised a highly interesting assortment of vehicles.

Most of Dodds' double-deckers came from English operators, such as this ex-Salford Corporation Leyland PD1A, seen on a Private Hire. (A.J. Douglas)

Negotiating a roundabout in the then New Town of East Kilbride, DRN 279, a Leyland PD2, joined the Dodds' ranks in 1965 from Ribble. The company's colours were red/cream or red/grey, but very often vehicles ran in the liveries of their previous owners. (A.J. Douglas)

Dodds also operated coaches, and 460 JRF, a Duple-bodied Commer, traverses Hamilton 'bottom' Cross. The corner confectioners' Birrell, later swallowed-up by R.S. McColl, along with the Hillman Minx and Wolseley cars following Dodds' vehicle, indicate an early-to-mid 1960s view. (A.J. Douglas)

Caught on camera minus a wheel in the yard at Lesmahagow, HCD 908 was a far-travelled Leyland PD1. This bus came to South Lanarkshire from Southdown, where it had been No.308 in that famous fleet. (A.J. Douglas)

John Dodds sold out to Wilson, Carnwath in December 1970, but continued driving for them on a part-time basis till he was seventy-three years of age.

Located in Forth, one of the county's outlying villages, Peter Tennant started his business way back in the early years of the twentieth century, hauling goods and people. Over the decades, both sides of the operation grew steadily, and Tennant became one of the longest-established transport providers for the Lanarkshire coalfields. Private Hire, Schools and other Contract work was also developed for an exceptionally varied and interesting fleet running in maroon and off-white colours.

In the yard at Forth, CDR 354 is best-described as a 'hybrid' bus. Originally ex-Plymouth, the Leyland TD7 chassis arrived via Lowland Motorways of Glasgow, and is seen wearing a Leyland body rebuilt by ECW from an old Central SMT Titan. (A.J. Douglas)

Pictured in Newmains near the end of its days in 1961, VD 7359 was a 1937 Leyland TS7 which had been given a new B32R body in 1951 by ECW, while with Central SMT as their T 102. (A.J. Douglas)

Seen outside a Kilmarnock cinema in 1964, DEK 46 was an Albion MR11 with forty-one-seat Plaxton coachwork. It was new in 1957 to J. Smith of Wigan. (A.J. Douglas)

Despite the illuminated 'PAYE.' sign, Tennant's didn't operate stage services in the time span of this book. One of a trio of Willowbrook-bodied Ford R114's bought from Trent Motor Services when still fairly young, MUP 696J is parked-up at Lanark after a school run.

Tennant's ceased their bus/coach operations in the late 1990s, but the haulage business remains a highy reputable, thriving company, still under family ownership, including the great-grandsons of Peter Tennant. (Photobus)

eleven

Bingo Buses!

Enjoying renewed popularity in the twenty-first century, the game of bingo reached its original peak from the late 1960s and through the following decade, when it was the housewives' choice of the ideal night out. One of Lanarkshire's larger halls which enjoyed big crowds (and big cash prizes) was the Alhambra, a former theatre on Main Street, Mossend, Bellshill.

To maintain the huge following, the owners, who also ran a 'sister' hall, The Plaza in Burnbank, provided transport for lotto-lovers from the neighbouring areas. For a few years, coaches were hired from Wilson McClure of Glenmavis, and an immaculate Daimler 'decker of Airdrie's James Wilson. As the demand increased, the Alhambra owners gambled on their own game of chance – they thought it would be more cost effective to buy and operate their own fleet of second-hand vehicles to ferry their patrons to the respective venues. Using the expertise of Tiger Coaches the dealers in nearby Salsburgh, the Bingorama bus operation commenced mid-1970s with an assortment of mainly double-deckers, all running in the colours of their former owners which included Fylde Corporation, Burnley & Pendle, Bury Corporation, J. Fishwick and Maidstone & District. Eventually, the Transport Manager 'standardised' by purchasing mostly ex-Central SMT vehicles, and Bristols in particular.

The livery was Kingfisher blue relieved by the original owners' cream, although in the latter years, the blue became dark. To comply with a non-PSV operation, no 'fares' could be taken, but a petty-cash box was in each vehicle into which bingo-ers popped their donations – basically a 'whip-round' for the driver, which effectively subsidised his wages. The fleet strength was always around the ten-twelve vehicles, and the operation continued into the 1980s, when ex-Glasgow Leyland Atlanteans were deployed along with surviving ex-Central Bristol FLFs, before 'House!' was called for a final time, as bingo lost its attraction. The once-grand Alhambra building has been demolished, replaced by a modern shop unit, but the adjoining café/fish-and-chip shop still survives!

Opposite above: A large, walled yard behind the Alhambra provided ample space for Bingorama's Bellshill base. Pictured here is a pair of ex-Central Lodekkas. Although showing GM 7629, this actually carried the body of B68, alongside B89. (K. Langhorn)

Opposite below: Nearest the camera is another Bristol LD. New in 1955 to Western SMT as their 1162, GCS 248 was acquired by Eastern Scottish in 1971, and as AA8 was painted in Baxter's livery. LWS 512 was an ex-LRT/Edinburgh Corporation Leyland PD2 with Metro-Cammell/Orion body. (K. Langhorn)

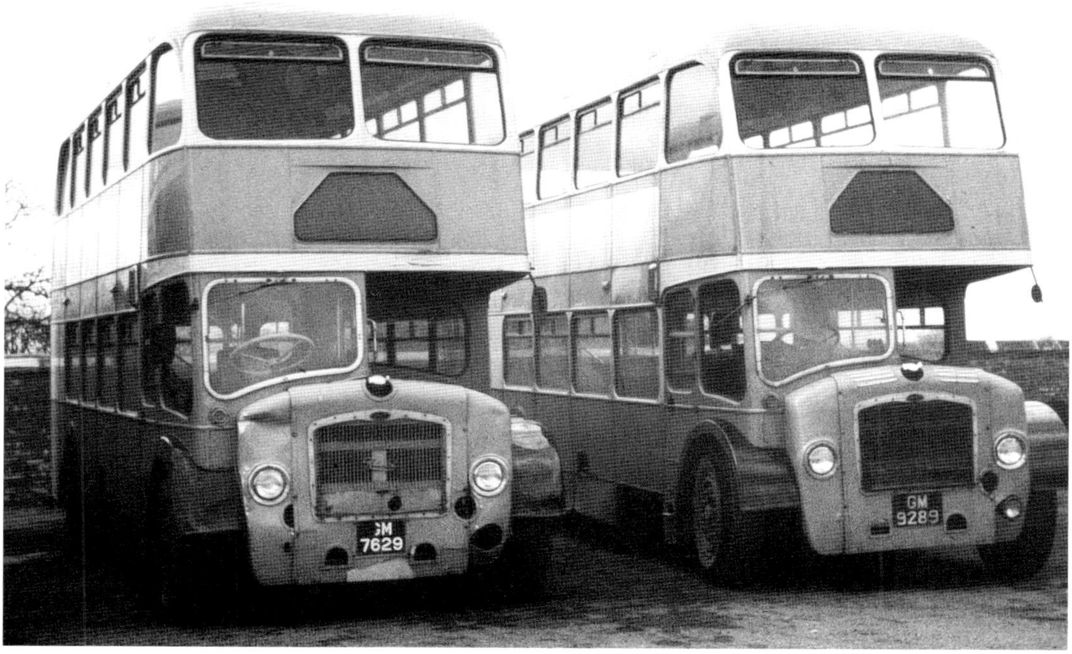
GM
7629
GM
9289

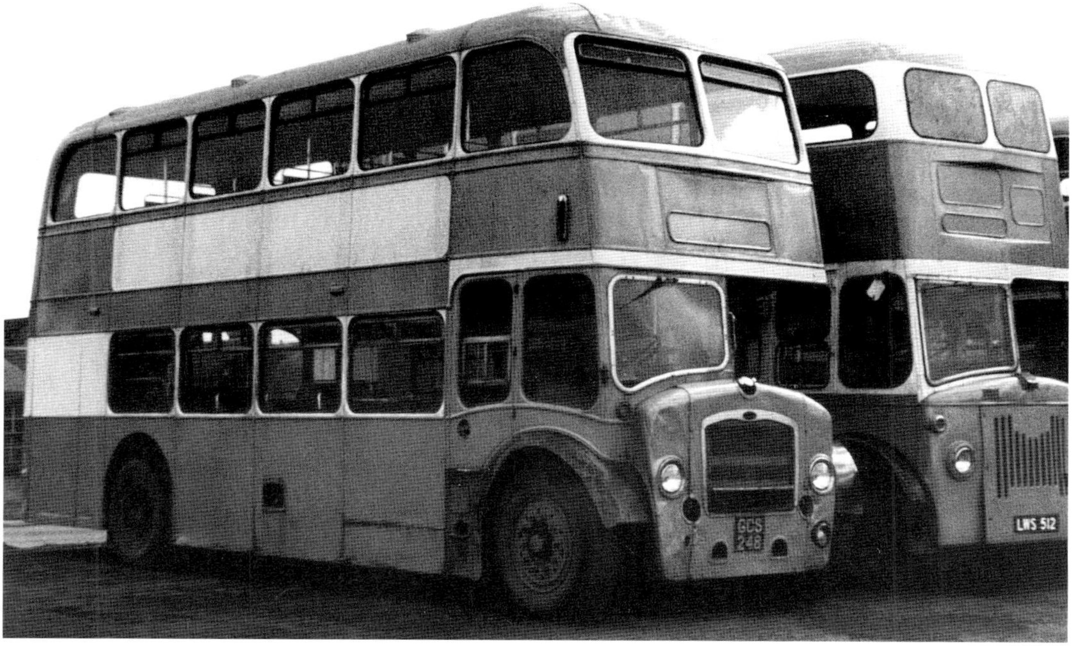
GCS
248
LWS 512

Above: 'Two Fat Ladies'... Captured in the darker livery, and still bearing their Central fleet-plates, this pair of FLFs await their passengers. Former BE 248 appears to have a problem with one half of the folding-leaf doors. (G. Stirling)

Left: Another former SBG vehicle was VMS 111J. A 1971 Leyland Leopard new to Alexander Midland as MPE 111, this single decker was traded-off to Central just four years later (T 269), in exchange for some of the Lanarkshire company's 'unwanted' Fleetlines. (D.G. MacDonald)